Java 9 Regular Exp

A hands-on guide to implement zero-length assertions, back-references, quantifiers, and many more

Anubhava Srivastava

BIRMINGHAM - MUMBAI

Java 9 Regular Expressions

First published: July 2017

Production reference: 1210717

Published by Packt Publishing Ltd.
Livery Place
35 Livery Street
Birmingham
B3 2PB, UK.
ISBN 978-1-78728-870-6

www.packtpub.com

Credits

Author
Anubhava Srivastava

Reviewer
Peter Verhas

Commissioning Editor
Merint Thomas Mathew

Acquisition Editor
Nitin Dasan

Content Development Editor
Vikas Tiwari

Technical Editor
Jijo Maliyekal

Copy Editor
Muktikant Garimella

Project Coordinator
Ulhas Kambali

Proofreader
Safis Editing

Indexer
Francy Puthiry

Graphics
Abhinash Sahu

Production Coordinator
Melwyn Dsa

About the Author

Anubhava Srivastava has more than 22 years of professional experience in architecture, design, and software development. He specializes mainly in the J2EE technology stack, web technologies, CICD, test-driven development, and AWS cloud-based development.

He is an active contributor to the Stack Overflow community. He currently stands in the top 35 users in terms of reputations out of the 7.5 million Stack Overflow users. He is passionate about regular expressions and is always willing to sharpen his regex skills further. He has answered close to 10,000 regex questions on Stack Overflow.

He has authored and released a test-driven framework, called GenericFixture, for FitNesse as an open source software. He maintains a technical blog at `http://anubhava.wordpress.com`

Anubhava can be found on LinkedIn at `https://www.linkedin.com/in/anubhava/`

You can follow him on Twitter at `@anubhava`.

First, I would like to express my gratitude toward the whole editing and publishing team at Packt Publishing for offering me an opportunity to write this book. Their support and guidance throughout this process encouraged me to explore more and dig deep.
This book would not have been possible without the support and encouragement of my wife and kids. I am really grateful to my family for trusting in my abilities and for understanding my long hours in front of the computer on weekends and holidays.
I want to acknowledge the immensely knowledgeable Stack Overflow contributors and open source community for teaching me advanced regex concepts.
Lastly, I want to say big thanks to my management team at AOL for allowing me to embark on this book writing journey in my off time.

About the Reviewer

Peter Verhas is a senior software engineer and software architect with a background in electrical engineering and economics. He pursued his MSc from TU Budapest and MBA from PTE Hungary. He has also studied at TU Delft and TU Vienna. He created his first programs in 1979, and since then, he has been the author of several open source programs. He has worked in the telecommunication and finance industries in several positions and was the CIO of the Hungarian startup, index.hu, during its initial days.

Peter works for EPAM Systems in Switzerland, participating in software development projects at various customer sites. He also supports talent acquisition by interviewing candidates and designs internal mentoring programs and training programs for developers.

Peter is the author of *Java 9 Programming by Example* and the co-author of *Mastering Java 9* by Packt.

You can follow Peter on Twitter at @verhas, LinkedIn, and GitHub. You can also read his technical blog, Java Deep, at http://javax0.wordpress.com.

www.PacktPub.com

For support files and downloads related to your book, please visit `www.PacktPub.com`.

Did you know that Packt offers eBook versions of every book published, with PDF and ePub files available? You can upgrade to the eBook version at `www.PacktPub.com`and as a print book customer, you are entitled to a discount on the eBook copy. Get in touch with us at `service@packtpub.com` for more details.

At `www.PacktPub.com`, you can also read a collection of free technical articles, sign up for a range of free newsletters and receive exclusive discounts and offers on Packt books and eBooks.

`https://www.packtpub.com/mapt`

Get the most in-demand software skills with Mapt. Mapt gives you full access to all Packt books and video courses, as well as industry-leading tools to help you plan your personal development and advance your career.

Why subscribe?

- Fully searchable across every book published by Packt
- Copy and paste, print, and bookmark content
- On demand and accessible via a web browser

Customer Feedback

Thanks for purchasing this Packt book. At Packt, quality is at the heart of our editorial process. To help us improve, please leave us an honest review on this book's Amazon page at https://www.amazon.com/dp/1787288706.

If you'd like to join our team of regular reviewers, you can e-mail us at customerreviews@packtpub.com. We award our regular reviewers with free eBooks and videos in exchange for their valuable feedback. Help us be relentless in improving our products!

Table of Contents

Preface

In today's information technology world, the size of data is growing by leaps and bounds. IT organizations are processing and storing huge amounts of textual data collected from various sources, such as user actions, leads, searches, shopping data, page views, page hits, and various other forms of user interactions. Search algorithms are used for parsing large texts to extract meaningful pertinent information. Regular expressions are the backbone of many such search algorithms.

Regular expressions (or regex in short) are everywhere these days. All the modern programming languages are shipped with a regex module or library to allow programmers to write regex-based programs. Regular expressions are a powerful tool in the programmer's toolbox and allow pattern matching. They are also used for manipulating text and data. This book will provide you with the know-how (and practical examples) to solve real-world problems using regex in Java.

This easy-to-follow regex book is a great place for you to familiarize yourself with the core concepts of regular expressions and to master their implementation with the new features of Java 9. You will learn to match, extract, and transform text by matching specific words, characters, and patterns. Readers will learn how to write efficient regular expressions for solving day-to-day problems involving text-based data.

What this book covers

Chapter 1, *Getting Started with Regular Expressions*, teaches what regular expressions are, what problems are best solved using regular expressions, and the rules to follow while writing them.

Chapter 2, *Understanding the Core Constructs of Java Regular Expressions*, covers quantifiers, anchors, boundary matchers, and all the available character classes and properties in Java. We will also learn Unicode text matching using regex in Java.

Chapter 3, *Working with Groups, Capturing, and References*, explores how to match and capture text in regex, the various types of groups available to us, the naming and numbering of a captured group, and how we should use back-reference for the captured groups.

Chapter 4, *Regular Expression Programming Using Java String and Scanner APIs*, introduces Java regex using Java String methods, and we will move on to regex capabilities in the Java Scanner API.

Chapter 5, *Introduction to Java Regular Expression APIs - Pattern and Matcher Classes*, discusses the dedicated Java APIs, java.util.regex.Pattern and java.util.regex.Matcher, for complete regex capabilities.

Chapter 6, *Exploring Zero-width Assertions, Lookarounds, and Atomic Groups*, focuses on zero-width assertions in regex. The chapter covers various zero-width assertions and their usages. We will then move on to learn the important topic of lookarounds in regex.

Chapter 7, *Understanding the Union, Intersection, and Subtraction of Character Classes*, says that the Java language has added the features of using the intersection and union of character classes in regex. This chapter covers these features.

Chapter 8, *Regular Expression Pitfalls, Optimization, and Performance Improvements*, explains how to test and optimize a poorly performing regex and various other performance tips.

What you need for this book

The software in this book was tested on Java version 9 on Ubuntu version 16.10. However, all the examples can also be run on the Windows and macOS X operating systems.

Who this book is for

This book is for Java developers who would like to understand and use regular expressions. If you are dealing with text processing problems, such as text validation, searching, and text manipulation, then learning regex is very important for you to make your job easier. This book does not expect readers to have any prior regex knowledge, since the book will cover every aspect of regex, starting from the absolute basics of regex. However, a basic knowledge of Java is assumed in order to be able to write and execute the example programs provided in the book.

Conventions

In this book, you will find a number of text styles that distinguish between different kinds of information. Here are some examples of these styles and an explanation of their meaning.

Code words in text, database table names, folder names, filenames, file extensions, pathnames, dummy URLs, user input, and Twitter handles are shown as follows: "The next lines of code read the link and assign it to the to the `BeautifulSoup` function."

A block of code is set as follows:

```
package example.regex;
public class StringMatches
{
   public static void main(String[] args)
}
```

When we wish to draw your attention to a particular part of a code block, the relevant lines or items are set in bold:

```
[default]
exten => s,1,Dial(Zap/1|30)
exten => s,2,Voicemail(u100)
exten => s,102,Voicemail(b100)
exten => i,1,Voicemail(s0)
```

Any command-line input or output is written as follows:

```
C:\Python34\Scripts> pip install –upgrade pip
C:\Python34\Scripts> pip install pandas
```

New terms and **important words** are shown in bold. Words that you see on the screen, for example, in menus or dialog boxes, appear in the text like this: "In order to download new modules, we will go to **Files** | **Settings** | **Project Name** | **Project Interpreter**."

Warnings or important notes appear like this.

Tips and tricks appear like this.

Reader feedback

Feedback from our readers is always welcome. Let us know what you think about this book-what you liked or disliked. Reader feedback is important for us as it helps us develop titles that you will really get the most out of.

To send us general feedback, simply e-mail `feedback@packtpub.com`, and mention the book's title in the subject of your message. If there is a topic that you have expertise in and you are interested in either writing or contributing to a book, see our author guide at `www.packtpub.com/authors`.

Customer support

Now that you are the proud owner of a Packt book, we have a number of things to help you to get the most from your purchase.

Downloading the example code

You can download the example code files for this book from your account at `http://www.packtpub.com`. If you purchased this book elsewhere, you can visit `http://www.packtpub.com/support` and register to have the files e-mailed directly to you.

You can download the code files by following these steps:

1. Log in or register to our website using your e-mail address and password.
2. Hover the mouse pointer on the **SUPPORT** tab at the top.
3. Click on **Code Downloads & Errata**.
4. Enter the name of the book in the **Search** box.
5. Select the book for which you're looking to download the code files.
6. Choose from the drop-down menu where you purchased this book from.
7. Click on **Code Download**.

Once the file is downloaded, please make sure that you unzip or extract the folder using the latest version of:

- WinRAR / 7-Zip for Windows
- Zipeg / iZip / UnRarX for Mac
- 7-Zip / PeaZip for Linux

The code bundle for the book is also hosted on GitHub at `https://github.com/PacktPubl ishing/Java-9-Regular-Expressions`. We also have other code bundles from our rich catalog of books and videos available at `https://github.com/PacktPublishing/`. Check them out!

Errata

Although we have taken every care to ensure the accuracy of our content, mistakes do happen. If you find a mistake in one of our books-maybe a mistake in the text or the code-we would be grateful if you could report this to us. By doing so, you can save other readers from frustration and help us improve subsequent versions of this book. If you find any errata, please report them by visiting `http://www.packtpub.com/submit-errata`, selecting your book, clicking on the **Errata Submission Form** link, and entering the details of your errata. Once your errata are verified, your submission will be accepted and the errata will be uploaded to our website or added to any list of existing errata under the Errata section of that title.

To view the previously submitted errata, go to `https://www.packtpub.com/books/conten t/support` and enter the name of the book in the search field. The required information will appear under the **Errata** section.

Piracy

Piracy of copyrighted material on the Internet is an ongoing problem across all media. At Packt, we take the protection of our copyright and licenses very seriously. If you come across any illegal copies of our works in any form on the Internet, please provide us with the location address or website name immediately so that we can pursue a remedy.

Please contact us at `copyright@packtpub.com` with a link to the suspected pirated material.

We appreciate your help in protecting our authors and our ability to bring you valuable content.

Questions

If you have a problem with any aspect of this book, you can contact us at `questions@packtpub.com`, and we will do our best to address the problem.

1
Getting Started with Regular Expressions

In this chapter, you will be introduced to regular expressions (or regex in short). You will learn about some real-world problems that can be solved by using regular expressions and the basic building blocks of regular expressions.

We will be covering the following topics in this chapter:

- Introduction to regular expressions
- A brief history of regular expressions
- The various flavors of regular expressions
- What type of problems need regular expressions to solve
- The basic rules of writing regular expressions
- Standard regular expression meta characters
- Basic regular expression examples

Introduction to regular expressions

Regular expression (or in short regex) is a very useful tool that is used to describe a search pattern for matching the text. Regex is nothing but a sequence of some characters that defines a search pattern. Regex is used for parsing, filtering, validating, and extracting meaningful information from large text, such as logs and output generated from other programs.

We find regular expressions in day-to-day use on many websites. For example, while searching for your favorite recipe on search engines, while filling up forms and entering data such as username and passwords, and so on. While setting up a password on many sites, we encounter password validation errors, such as password must contain one digit or at least one uppercase letter or at least one special character, and so on. All these checks can be done using regular expressions. A few more typical examples of regular expressions are validating phone numbers or validating postal/zip/pin codes.

A bit of history of regular expressions

Renowned mathematician Stephen Kleene built a model in the year 1956 using finite automata for simple algebra. He described regular languages using his mathematical notation called *regular sets*. Computer programmers started using regular expressions in the 1970s when the Unix operating system and some of its text editors and text processing utilities such as ed, sed, emacs, lex, vi, grep, awk, and so on were built. Regular expressions gained more popularity with the arrival of Perl and Tcl scripting languages in the 1980s and 1990s. Since then, all the popular programming languages, such as Java, Python, Ruby, R, PHP, and .NET have built very good support of regular expressions.

Various flavors of regular expressions

All the programming and scripting languages have built-in support for regular expressions these days. The basic rules to define and execute regular expressions are pretty much the same across all the languages. However, these regex implementations have their own flavors that differ from each other at the advanced level. We will cover regular expressions using Java in this book.

Some of the popular flavors of regular expressions are as follows:

- .NET
- Java
- Perl
- PCRE (PHP)
- JavaScript
- VBScript
- Python
- R
- Ruby

- std::regex
- boost::regex
- **Basic Regular Expressions** (**BRE**) - used by Unix utilities ed, vi, sed, grep, and so on
- **Extended Regular Expressions** (**ERE**) - used by Unix utilities sed, grep, awk, and so on

What type of problems need regular expressions to solve

Some programmers wonder why they even need to learn regular expressions. Here are some use cases:

- While searching for some text at times, there are cases where we don't know the value of the text upfront. We just know some rules or patterns of the text. For example, searching for a MAC address in a log message, searching for IP address in a web server access log, or searching for a 10-digit mobile number that may be optionally preceded by `0` or `+<2 digit country code>`.
- Sometimes, the length of the text we are trying to extract is unknown, for example, searching URLs that start with `http://` or `https://` in a CSV file.
- Sometimes, we need to split a given text on delimiters of a variable type and length and generate tokens.
- Sometimes, we need to extract text that falls between two or more search patterns.
- Often, we need to validate the various forms of user inputs, such as bank account number, passwords, usernames, credit card info, phone number, date of birth, and so on.
- There are situations where you only want to capture all the repeated words from a line.
- To convert input text into certain predefined formats, such as inserting a comma after every three digits or removing commas inside parentheses only.
- To do a global search replace while skipping all the escaped characters.

The basic rules of regular expressions

Many of you are familiar with wild cards (in the Unix world, it is called **glob pattern**) matching of text. Here:

- **?** matches any single character
- ***** matches any sequence of characters
- **[abc]** matches any one character inside square brackets, so it will match a, b, or c

The regular expression pattern goes many steps farther than wild cards, where one can set many rules in a regex pattern, such as the following:

- Match a character or a group of characters optionally (0 or 1 times)
- Use quantifiers in regex patterns to match variable length text
- Use a character class to match one of the listed characters or match a range of characters
- Use a negated character class to match any character except those matched by the character class
- Match only certain character categories, such as match only digits, only upper case letters, or only punctuation characters
- Match a character or a group of characters for a specific length.
- Match a length range, such as allow only six to 10 digits in the input or match an input of a minimum of eight characters
- Use Boolean "OR" in an alternation to match one of the few alternative options
- Use groups in regex patterns and capture substrings that we want to extract or replace from a given input
- Alter the behavior of matching by keeping it greedy (eager), lazy (reluctant), or possessive
- Use back references and forward references of groups that we capture
- Use zero-width assertions such as the following:
  - Start and end anchors
  - Word boundary
  - Lookahead and lookbehind assertions
  - Start a match from the end of a previous match

For example, in a regex to match a or b we can use the following alternation:

```
a|b
```

To match one or more instances of the digit 5, we can use the following:

```
5+
```

To match any substring that starts with p and ends with w, we can use the following:

```
p.*w
```

Constructs of the standard regular expression and meta characters

Let's get familiar with core constructs of regular expressions and some reserve meta characters that have a special meaning in regular expressions. We shall cover these constructs in detail in the coming chapters:

Symbol	Meaning	Example
. (dot or period)	Matches any character other than newline.	Matches #, @, **A**, **f**, **5**, or .
* (asterisk)	* matches zero or more occurrences of the preceding character or group.	**m*** matches 0 or more occurrences of the letter **m**.
+ (plus)	+ matches one or more occurrences of the preceding element.	**m+** matches one or more occurrences of the letter **m**.
? (question mark)	? means optional match. It is used to match zero or one occurrence of the preceding element. It is also used for lazy matching (which will be covered in the coming chapters).	**nm?** means match **n** or **nm**, as **m** is an **optional** match here.
| (pipe)	| means alternation. It is used to match one of the elements separated by |	**m|n|p** means match either the letter **m** or the letter **n** or the letter **p**
^ (cap)	^ is called anchor, that matches start of the line	^m matches m only when it is the first character of the string that we are testing against the regular expression. Also, note that you do not use ^ in the middle of a regular expression.

$ (dollar)	$ is called anchor that matches line end.	m$ matches m only at line end.
\b (backslash followed by the letter b)	Alphabets, numbers, and underscore are considered word characters. \b asserts word boundary, which is the position just before and after a word.	\bjava\b matches the word, java . So, it will not match javascript since the word, javascript, will fail to assert \b after java in the regex.
\B (backslash followed by uppercase B)	\B asserts true where \b doesn't, that is, between two word characters.	For the input text, *abc*, \B will be asserted at two places: • Between *a* and *b*. • Between *b* and *c*.
(...) a sub-pattern inside round parentheses	This is for grouping a part of text that can be used to capture a certain substring or for setting precedence.	m(ab)*t matches m, followed by zero or more occurrences of the substring, **ab**, followed by **t**.
{min,max}	A quantifier range to match the preceding element between the minimum and the maximum number.	mp{2,4} matches m followed 2 to 4 occurrences of the letter p.
[...]	This is called a character class.	[A–Z] matches any uppercase English alphabet.
\d (backslash followed by the letter d)	This will match any digit.	\d matches any digit in the 0-9 range.
\D (backslash followed by uppercase D)	This matches any character that is not a digit.	\D matches a, $, or _.
\s (backslash followed by the letter s)	Matches any whitespace, including tab, space, or newline.	\s matches [\t\n].
\S (backslash followed by uppercase S)	Matches any non-whitespace.	\S matches the opposite of \s
\w (backslash followed by the letter w)	Matches any word character that means all alphanumeric characters or underscore.	\w will match [a-zA-Z0-9_], so it will match any of these strings: "*abc*", "*a123*", or "*pq_12_ABC*"

\W (backslash followed by the letter W)	Matches any non-word character, including whitespaces. In regex, any character that is not matched by \w can be matched using \W.	It will match any of these strings: "+/=", "$", or " !~"

Some basic regular expression examples

Let's look at some basic examples of regular expressions:

```
ab*c
```

This will match a, followed by zero or more b, followed by c.

```
ab+c
```

This will match a followed by one or more b, followed by c.

```
ab?c
```

This will match a followed by zero or one b, followed by c. Thus, it will match both abc or ac.

```
^abc$
```

This will match abc in a line, and the line must not have anything other than the string abc due to the use of the start and end anchors on either side of the regex.

```
a(bc)*z
```

This will match a, followed by zero or more occurrences of the string bc, followed by z. Thus, it will match the following strings: az, abcz, abcbcz, abcbcbcz, and so on.

```
ab{1,3}c
```

This will match a, followed by one to three occurrences of b, followed by c. Thus, it will match following strings: abc, abbc, and abbbc.

```
red|blue
```

This will match either the string red or the string blue.

```
\b(cat|dog)\b
```

This will match either the string `cat` or the string `dog`, ensuring both `cat` and `dog` must be complete words; thus, it will **fail** the match if the input is `cats` or `dogs`.

```
[0-9]
```

This is a character class with a character range. The preceding example will match a digit between 0 and 9.

```
[a-zA-Z0-9]
```

This is a character class with a character range. The preceding example will match any alpha-numeric character.

```
^\d+$
```

This regex will match an input containing only one or more digits.

```
^\d{4,8}$
```

This regex will allow an input containing four to eight digits only. For example, 1234, 12345, 123456, and 12345678 are valid inputs.

```
^\d\D\d$
```

This regex not only allows only one digit at the start and end but also enforces that between these two digits there must be one non-digit character. For example, 1-5, 3:8, 8X2, and so on are valid inputs.

```
^\d+\.\d+$
```

This regex matches a floating point number. For example, 1.23, 1548.567, and 7876554.344 are valid inputs.

```
.+
```

This matches any character one or more times. For example, qwqewe, 12233, or f5^h_=!bg are all valid inputs:

```
^\w+\s+\w+$
```

This matches a word, followed by one or more whitespaces, followed by another word in an input. For example, `hello word`, `John Smith`, and `United Kingdom` will be matched using this regex.

Engine is a term often used for an underlying module that evaluates the provided regular expression and matches the input string.

Eager matching

At this point, it is important to understand one important behavior of regular expression engines, called eagerness. A regular expression engine performs a match operation from left to right in an input string. While matching a regex pattern against the input string, the regex engine moves from left to right and is always eager to complete a match, even though there are other alternative ways in the regular expression to complete the match. Once a substring is matched, it stops proceeding further and returns the match. Only when a character position fails to match all the possible permutations of the regular expression, then the regex engine moves character by character to attempt a match at the next position in the input string. While evaluating a regex pattern, the regex engine may move backwards (backtrack) one position at a time to attempt matching.

The effect of eager matching on regular expression alternation

This regular expression engine behavior may return unexpected matches in alternation if alternations are not ordered carefully in the regex pattern.

Take an example of this regex pattern, which matches the strings `white` or `whitewash`:

```
white|whitewash
```

While applying this regex against an input of *whitewash*, the regex engine finds that the first alternative `white` matches the *white* substring of the input string *whitewash*, hence, the regex engine stops proceeding further and returns the match as `white`.

Note that our regex pattern has a better second alternative as `whitewash`, but due to the regex engine's eagerness to complete and return the match, the first alternative is returned as a match and the second alternative is ignored.

However, consider swapping the positions of the third and fourth alternatives in our regex pattern to make it as follows:

```
whitewash|white
```

If we apply this against the same input, *whitewash,* then the regex engine correctly returns the match as whitewash.

We can also use anchors or boundary matchers in our regular expressions to make it match a complete word. Any of the following two patterns will match and return whitewash as a match:

```
^(white|whitewash)$
```

```
\b(white|whitewash)\b
```

Let's take a look at a more interesting example, which attempts to match a known literal string *"cat & rat"* or a complete word in the input, using the following pattern:

```
\b(\w+|cat & rat)\b
```

If the input string is *story of cat & rat,* and we apply our regex pattern repeatedly, then the following four matched substrings will be returned:

```
1. story
2. of
3. cat
4. rat
```

It is because the regex engine is eagerly using the first alternative pattern \w+ to match a complete word and is returning all the matched words. The engine never attempts a second alternative of the literal string, cat & rat, because a successful match is always found using the first alternative. However, let's change the regex pattern to the following:

```
\b(cat & rat|\w+)\b
```

If we apply this regex on the same sting, *story of cat & rat,* and we apply our regex pattern repeatedly, then the following three matched substrings will be returned:

```
1. story
2. of
3. cat & rat
```

This is because now cat & rat is the first alternative and when the regex engine moves to a position before the letter c in the input, it is able to match and return a successful match using the first alternative.

Summary

In this chapter, you were introduced to regular expressions with a bit of history and their flavors. You learnt some use cases where regex are needed. Finally, we covered the basic rules and building blocks of writing regex, with a few examples. You also learnt the eager-matching behavior of the regex engine and how it may impact matching in alternations.

In the next chapter, we will go a level deeper and cover the core concepts of regex in detail, such as quantifiers, lazy vs greedy matching, anchors, negated character classes, Unicode and predefined character classes, special escape sequences, and the rules of escaping inside a character class.

2
Understanding the Core Constructs of Java Regular Expressions

Using Java as a regular expression flavor, in this chapter, we will go a bit deeper and learn in detail about anchors, quantifiers, boundary matchers, all the available character classes, negated character classes, predefined character classes, and character classes escaping rules, using Java as a reference point. You will also learn Unicode text matching, using *regular expressions* in Java. We will also cover greedy versus non-greedy (lazy matching) and the change of regular expression behavior with lazy matching.

We will cover the following topics in this chapter:

- Anchors and quantifiers
- Boundary matchers
- Character classes
- Regex escaping rules
- Escaping inside character classes
- Negated character classes
- Predefined character classes
- Unicode characters matching
- Greedy quantifiers
- Lazy quantifiers
- Possessive quantifiers
- Various embedded modes in regular expressions and their meaning
- Enabling/disabling regular expression modes inside the regex

Understanding the core constructs of regular expressions

Certain special character constructs are allowed literally in Java regular expressions. Here they are:

Special Character	Meaning
\0c	A character with the octal value c
\0cc	A character with the octal value cc
\0ncc	A character with the octal value ncc, where n cannot be more than 3
\xhh	A character with the hexadecimal value 0xhh
\uhhhh	A character with the hexadecimal value 0xhhhh
\x{h...h}	A character with the hexadecimal value 0xh...h, where h must be a valid CODE_POINT
\n	Newline character or u000A
\t	Tab character or u0009
\r	Carriage return character or u000D
\f	Form feed character or u000C
\e	Escape character or u\u001B
\a	Bell character or \u0007
\cn	A control character represented by n

Quantifiers

We briefly looked at quantifiers in the first chapter. Quantifiers allow us to quantify the occurrences of our matches. We can match the input in various ways, such as an optional match, an open-ended range, a closed range, and by using a fixed number. Let's take a closer look at them, as quantifiers are integral to most of the regular expressions.

Basic quantifiers

The following table lists all the quantifiers available in Java regular expressions:

Quantifier	Meaning
m*	Match **m** zero or more times
m+	Match **m** one or more times
m?	Match **m** one or zero times (also called an optional match)
m{X}	Match **m** exactly X times
m{X,}	Match **m** X or more times
m{X,Y}	Match **m** at least X and at most Y times

In all the aforementioned cases, **m** can be a single character or a *group* of characters. We will discuss grouping in more detail later.

Examples using quantifiers

Let's look at few examples to understand these basic quantifiers better.

Which regex pattern should be used to match a two-digit year or a four-digit year?

    \d{2}|\d{4}

Which regex pattern should be used to match a signed decimal number? The pattern should also match a signed integer number:

    ^[+-]?\d*\.?\d+$

Here is the breakup of the preceding regex pattern:

- The ^ and $ symbols are the start/end anchors
- The [+-]? pattern makes either the + sign or the - sign (optional because of ?) at the start
- The \d* pattern matches zero or more digits
- The \.? pattern matches an optional dot (.) literally
- The \d+ pattern matches one or more digits

The preceding regex will match all of these inputs:

- `.45`
- `123789`
- `5`
- `123.45`
- `+67.66`
- `-987.34`

What would be the regex to match a number that is at least 10 but not more than 9999?

`^\d{2,4}$`

Since we have a minimum of two digits, 10 is the smallest match, whereas the maximum number of digits allowed is four, and hence, 9999 is the highest match.

What is the regex for an input that has seven digits and that can have + or – at the start?

`^[+-]?\d{7}$`

The `[+-]?` pattern makes it an optional match at the start before we match the seven digits using `\d{7}`.

 The preceding regex can also be written as `^[+-]?[0-9]{7}$`, as `\d` is a shorthand property to match `[0-9]`

Greedy versus reluctant (lazy) matching using quantifiers

So far, we have discussed all the quantifiers available to us in a regular expression to match fixed-size or variable-length text. These quantifiers are, by default, **greedy** in nature. Greediness is in terms of their matching. In a regex, quantifiers attempt to match the longest possible text, from left to right. Only when the regex engine fails to complete a match, it moves back in the input text one character at a time, as required, to complete the match. Sometimes, the regex engine moves back and forth multiple times in attempts to complete a match in a complex (nested) regular expression.

So, for example, if the input is `pqrstmprt` and our regular expression is `p.+r`, then our match will be from `p` at the start to the last `r`, that is, `pqrstmpr`, not `pqr`. It is due to the same greediness that was stated earlier, where the regex engine attempts to match the longest possible match when using quantifiers.

Regular expressions also provide a way to change this greedy behavior of the regex engine. If we place a `?` (*called the lazy or reluctant quantifier*) in front of any of the quantifiers, then the behavior of the regex engine changes from **greedy** to **lazy**. With the lazy quantifier in place, the regex engine attempts to match the shortest match, only expanding further as required to complete the match with the remainder of the regex pattern next to the lazy quantifier.

So, in the preceding example, if we use the regex as `p.+?r`, then our matched text will be `pqr`, because *pqr* is the smallest possible match between `p` and `r`.

Here is a list of all the greedy quantifiers and their corresponding lazy quantifiers:

Greedy Quantifier	Lazy Quantifier
m*	m*?
m+	m+?
m?	m??
m{X}	m{X}?
m{X,}	m{X,}?
m{X,Y}	m{X,Y}?

Possessive quantifiers

Possessive quantifiers are quantifiers that are greedy when matching text like greedy quantifiers do. Both greedy and possessive quantifiers try to match as many characters as possible. The important difference, however, is that the possessive quantifiers do not backtrack (go back) unlike greedy quantifiers; therefore, it is possible that the regex match fails if the possessive quantifiers go too far.

This table shows all the three types of quantifiers, side by side:

Greedy Quantifier	Lazy Quantifier	Possessive Quantifier
m*	m*?	m*+
m+	m+?	m++
m?	m??	m?+
m{X}	m{X}?	m{X}+
m{X,}	m{X,}?	m{X,}+
m{X,Y}	m{X,Y}?	m{X,Y}+

Let's take an example input string, a1b5, and see the behavior of the greedy, lazy, and possessive quantifiers.

If we apply a regex using the greedy quantifier, \w+\d, then it will match a1b (the longest match before backtracking starts) using \w+, and 5 will be matched using \d; thus, the full match will be a1b5.

Now, if we apply a regex using the non-greedy quantifier, \w+?\d, then it will match a (the shortest match before expanding starts) using \w+?, and then the adjacent digit 1 will be matched using \d. Thus, the first full match will be a1. If we let the regex execute again, then it will find another match, b5.

Finally, if we apply a regex using the possessive quantifier, \w++\d, then it will match all the characters a1b5 (the longest possible match without giving back) using \w++ . Due to this, \d remains unmatched, and hence the regex fails to find any match.

Let's take another example. The requirement is to match a string that starts with lowercase English alphabets or hyphen. The string can have any character after the alphabets/hyphens, except a colon. There can be any number of any characters of any length after the colon until the end.

An example of a valid input is as-df999 and that of an invalid input is asdf-:123.

Now, let's try solving this regex problem using a greedy quantifier regex:

```
^[a-z-]+[^:].*$
```

Unfortunately, this is not the right regex pattern because this regex will match both the aforementioned valid and invalid inputs. This is because of the backtracking behavior of the regex engine in greedy quantifiers. The `[a-z-]+` pattern will find the longest possible match in the form of `asdf-`, but due to the negated character class pattern `[^:]`, the regex engine will backtrack one position to `asdf` and will match the next *hyphen* for `[^:]`. All the remaining text, that is, `:123`, will be matched using `.*`.

Let's try to solve this regex problem using the following possessive quantifier regex:

    ^[a-z-]++[^:].*$

This regex pattern will still match our valid input, but it will fail to match an invalid input because there is no backtracking in possessive quantifiers; hence, the regex engine will not go back any position after matching `asdf-` in the second example string. Since the next character is a colon and our regex sub-pattern is `[^:]`, the regex engine will stop matching and correctly declare our invalid input a failed match.

Possessive quantifiers are good for the performance of the underlying regex engine because the engine does not have to keep any backtracking information in memory. The performance increase is even more when a regex fails to match because possessive quantifiers fail faster. So, remember that the benefit of possessive quantifiers is to improve the regex performance, especially when using nested quantifiers.

Boundary constructs

Boundary constructs allow us to specify where our matches should start or stop by restricting our matches to certain boundaries. We avoid matching unwanted text by adding restrictions to the start and stop positions of the matching text using boundary matchers. Here are all the boundary constructs available in Java regular expressions:

Boundary Matcher Name	Meaning
\b	Word boundary; position between a word and a non-word character
\B	Non-word boundary; it compliments \b and asserts true wherever \b asserts false
^	Line-start anchor, which matches the start of a line
$	Line-end anchor, which matches just before the optional line break at the end of a line

\A	Permanent start of input; in a multiline input using MULTILINE mode, \A matches only at the very beginning, while ^ is matched at every line start position
\z	Permanent end of input; in a multiline input using MULTILINE mode, \z matches only at the very end while $ is matched at every line end position
\Z	Similar to \z with the only difference being that it matches just before the optional line break at the very end of the input.
\G	End of the previous match; we will discuss it in advanced sections of the book in the next chapters.

Let's recall from the first chapter that [a-zA-Z0-9_] are called word characters. All other characters are considered non-word characters.

Examples using boundary constructs

Which regex should be used to match "at" when the input is 'Hat at work"?

    \bat\b

The preceding regex should be used because \b (word boundary) stops the regex engine to match at in Hat, because \bat\b can match full words only.

What should be regex if we only want to match at in Hat but not the one that was matched in the preceding regex?

    \Bat\b

Now, this regex will match at that is a part of Hat because \B asserts a position that is between two word characters or a position between two non-word characters. Because of the presence of \B in the regex, it matches at only in Hat but not the word at.

If the input is suppress expression press depression, what will be the matches if the regex is \Bpress\B?

    suppress ex**press**ion press de**press**ion

This is because \B matches the position between word characters, and the other instances, suppress and press, have non-word characters after press.

If the input is `ppp\n555\n`, then show the matched text using the following two regular expressions:

- `\Ap+\n5{3}\Z`
- `\Ap+\n5{3}\z`

Here are the matches:

A) `ppp\n555`
B) `No match`

The starting part, `\Ap+\n5{3}`, is common in both the regex patterns and matches `ppp\n555` both the times. However, we are getting `no match` in the second case because of the subtle difference between the `\Z` and `\z` assertions. `\Z` asserts the position at the end or just before the last line terminator whereas `\z` always asserts the position at the very end. Due to the presence of `\n` at the end of the file, our second regex does not match. If we change the second regex to `\Ap+\n5{3}\n\z`, then it will match the entire input.

 Note that the end anchor `$` also behaves like `\z` if the *MULTILINE flag (will be discussed later)* is not enabled in an input text with multiple lines. Thus, the preceding input string can also be matched using `^p+\n5{3}$`.

Character classes

We briefly looked at character classes in the first chapter. Character classes (or character sets) let us match one out of the many characters defined inside a class. Character classes are enclosed inside a square bracket. The order of the characters inside a character class does not matter.

Examples of character classes

Which regex will match the letters *p, m,* or *z*?

Solution 1:

    [pmz]

Solution 2:

    [zmp]

Solution 3:

```
[mzp]
```

All the preceding three regular expressions will behave in exactly the same manner because the order of the characters inside the character class does not matter.

Which regex will match English language vowels *a*, *e*, *i*, *o*, and *u*?

```
[aeiou]
```

Which regex will match the field extensions .mp3 or .mp3?

```
\.mp[34]
```

Which regex will match the letters @, #, or =?

```
[@#=]
```

Range inside a character class

We can also specify a **character range** inside a character class by using a hyphen (–) between two characters. You just have to make sure that the left-hand side character of a range is lower in the ASCII table than the right-hand side character. We can match all the digits using the regex patterns, [0123456789], or a shorter [0-9].

Examples of character range

The following is a regex that matches any uppercase or lowercase alphabet in the English language:

```
[a-zA-Z]
```

The a-z pattern is for the lowercase character range and A-Z is for the uppercase character range.

The following regex matches any alphanumeric characters:

```
[a-zA-Z0-9]
```

Alpha numeric characters consist of any English alphabets and digits.

The following regex matches any hexadecimal character:

```
[a-fA-F0-9]
```

We know that hexadecimal characters consist of digits, 0 to 9, and letters, A to F (ignore casing). The preceding regex pattern shows a character class that includes these two character ranges. We use a-f and A-F ranges to make it match uppercase or lowercase letters.

Escaping special regex metacharacters and escaping rules inside the character classes

We know that . matches any character, [and] are used for character classes, { and } are used for limiting quantifiers, and ? , *, and + are used for various quantifiers. To match any of the metacharacters *literally*, one needs to *escape* these characters using a *backslash* (\ ) to suppress their special meaning. Similarly, ^ and $ are anchors that are also considered regex metacharacters.

Let's see some examples of escaping metacharacters in regular expressions.

The following regex matches the string, a.b?:

```
a\.b\?
```

The following regex matches the string, {food}:

```
\{food\}
```

The following regex matches the string, abc:][ ]{{:

```
abc:\]\[\}\{
```

The following regex matches the string, $25.50:

```
\$\d+\.\d+
```

The following regex matches the string, ^*+.:

```
\^\*\+\.
```

Escaping inside a character class

In the Java regex engine, all the special regex metacharacters lose their special meaning inside a character class except the ^ (**carrot**), – (**hyphen**),] (**right square bracket**), and \ (**backslash**) characters.

Inside a character class, the hyphen also does not need to be escaped when used as the first or last character, since a character range requires both the left-hand side and the right-hand side characters. Similarly, ^ (carrot) needs to escaped only when used as the first character inside a character class.

Examples of escaping rules inside the character class

The following regex matches a string containing one or more of the `ap.9` characters:

```
^[ap9.]+$
```

The dot (`.`) doesn't need to be escaped inside the character class.

The following regex matches a string containing one or more of the `@#$%.*` characters:

```
^[$#@%.*]+$
```

None of the preceding special characters require escaping inside the character class.

The following regex matches a string containing one or more of the `?*+.` characters:

```
^[*+?.]+$
```

The following regex matches an input that allows any digit, `]`, or `^` in the input:

```
^[\^\]0-9]+$
```

We can also write our regex as `^[\]0-9^]+$` by moving `^` away from the first position and avoiding the escaping.

The following regex matches an input that allows any alphanumeric character, hyphen, dot, or backslash, such as `xyzTR-4.5\00`:

```
^[a-zA-Z0-9.\-\\]+$
```

We can also write our regex as follows by moving `-` to the last position inside the character class, thus avoiding the escaping:

```
^[a-zA-Z0-9.\\-]+$
```

Literally matching a string that may contain special regex metacharacters

We have seen how we need to escape all the special regex metacharacters to be able to match them literally.

The Java regex engine provides special escape sequences, \Q and \E, for this purpose. Any string that is wrapped between \Q and \E looses interpretation of all the regex metacharacters in the wrapped string.

For example, to write a regex that matches a string ^*+., we can avoid all escaping and use this regex:

    \Q^*+.\E

Note that there must not be any character escaping between \Q and \E sequences.

To match an input string, "[a-z0-9]", we can write our regex as follows:

    \Q[a-z0-9]\E

Java provides a convenient method to return a literal pattern sting for the given string called `Pattern.quote(String)`. We will learn about this method in Chapter 5, *Introduction to Java Regular Expressions APIs - Pattern and Matcher Classes*, of the book.

Negated character classes

By placing the carrot character (^) in the first position inside a character class (just next to [) **negates** the matching of the character class. A negated character class matches any character that is not included in the class. A negated character class also negates a character range by matching any character not matched by the character range.

You learned in Chapter 1, *Getting Started with Regular Expressions*, that dot (.) matches any character except the newline character. However, note that the negated character class also matches newline characters such as \r, \n, and so on.

Examples of negated character classes

The following regex matches any character except a forward slash:

    [^/]

Also, remember the fact that a negated character such as `[^/]` must match a single character. It doesn't match zero-width assertions such as `^`, `$`, `\Z`, `\z`, `\b`, `\B`, and so on.

The following regex matches any character but a and A:

```
[^aA]
```

The following regex matches all the *consonants* of the English language:

```
[^aeiou]
```

All non-vowels are considered *consonants*; hence, we just need to negate the vowel character class.

The following regex matches all the characters except digits, dots, and line breaks:

```
[^0-9.\r\n]
```

In this regex, we could also use the predefined property \d for [0-9]:

```
[^\d.\r\n]
```

This regex matches `http` followed by any character except `s`:

```
http[^s]
```

Predefined shorthand character classes

As we have seen from the preceding examples, certain character classes, such as digits `[0-9]` or word characters `[0-9A-Za-z_]`, are used in most regex patterns. The Java language, like all regular expression flavors, provides convenient predefined character classes for these character classes. Here is the list:

Shorthand Class	Meaning	Character Class
\d	A digit 0-9	`[0-9]`
\D	A non-digit	`[^\d]`
\w	A word character	`[a-zA-Z0-9_]`
W	A non-word character	`[^\w]`

\s	A whitespace character, including line break	`[ \t\r\n\f\x0B]`
\S	A non-whitespace chacracter	`[^\s]`
\h	A horizontal whitespace character	`[ \t\xA0\u1680\u180e\u2000-\u200a\u202f\u205f\u3000]`
\H	A non-horizontal whitespace character	`[^\h]`
\v	A vertical whitespace character	`[\n\x0B\f\r\x85\u2028\u2029]`
\V	A non-vertical whitespace character	`[^\v]`

POSIX character classes

Java also supports many POSIX character classes for matching ASCII text. Here is the list:

POSIX Character Class	Meaning	Character Class
\p{ASCII}	All ASCII characters	`[\x00-\x7F]`
\p{Digit}	Any digit	`[0-9]`
\p{Lower}	Lowercase alphabets	`[a-z]`
\p{Upper}	Uppercase alphabets	`[A-Z]`
\p{Alpha}	Any alphabet	`[\p{Lower}\p{Upper}]`
\p{Alnum}	Any alpha-numeric character	`[\p{Lower}p{Upper}\p{Digit}]`
\p{Punct}	A punctuation character	`[!"\#$%&'()*+,-./:;<=>?@\[\\\]^_`{|}~]`

\p{Blank}	Space or tab	[\t]
\p{Space}	A whitespace character	[\t\n\x0B\f\r]
\p{Graph}	A visible ASCII character	[\p{Alnum}\p{Punct}]
\p{Print}	A printable character	[\p{Graph}\x20]
\p{Cntrl}	A control character	[\x00-\x1F\x7F]
\p{XDigit}	A hexadecimal digit	[0-9a-fA-F]

Java also supports four additional predefined character classes based on the `java.lang.Character` methods:

Class Name	Implementing Method
\p{javaLowerCase}	Equivalent to `java.lang.Character.isLowerCase()`
\p{javaUpperCase}	Equivalent to `java.lang.Character.isUpperCase()`
\p{javaWhitespace}	Equivalent to `java.lang.Character.isWhitespace()`
\p{javaMirrored}	Equivalent to `java.lang.Character.isMirrored()`

Unicode support in Java regular expressions

So far, all the examples that we have seen in the first two chapters are for the English language only. However, a regular expression needs to have full support for all the languages using Unicode characters. Java has a Unicode-based regex engine and has extensive support for various Unicode scripts, blocks, and categories.

A specific Unicode character can be matched in two different ways in Java:

1. **Unicode escape sequence or the** `\u` **notation**: This can be written as `"\u1234"` or `"\\u1234"`.
2. **Hex notation**: This can be written as `"\x{1234}"`.

Commonly used Unicode character properties

Here is the list of commonly used Unicode character properties in regular expressions that require to match Unicode texts:

Unicode character class	Meaning
\p{L}	Match any letter from any language
\p{Lu}	Match any uppercase letter from any language
\p{Ll}	Match any lowercase letter from any language
\p{N}	Match any digit from any language
\p{P}	Match any punctuation letter from any language
\p{Z}	Match any kind of whitespace or invisible separator
\p{C}	Match any invisible control letter
\p{Sc}	Match any currency symbol
\R	Any Unicode linebreak sequence; is equivalent to `\u000D\u000A|[\u000A\u000B\u000C\u000D\u0085\u2028\u2029]` **It is recommended to use** `\R` **to match any newline character even if dealing with ASCII text.**

Negation of the preceding regex directives

To match a single character belonging to a particular *category*, we use the `\p{propertyName}` directive.

To match a single character **not** belonging to a particular *category*, we use the `\P{propertyName}` directive (note the uppercase **P** instead of the lowercase **p**).

Unicode scripts support

Java supports all the Unicode scripts as defined by the Unicode standard. Here is a list of all the supported Unicode scripts:

- `\p{IsCommon}`
- `\p{IsArabic}`
- `\p{IsArmenian}`
- `\p{IsBengali}`
- `\p{IsBopomofo}`
- `\p{IsBraille}`

- \p{IsBuhid}
- \p{IsCanadian_Aboriginal}
- \p{IsCherokee}
- \p{IsCyrillic}
- \p{IsDevanagari}
- \p{IsEthiopic}
- \p{IsGeorgian}
- \p{IsGreek}
- \p{IsGujarati}
- \p{IsGurmukhi}
- \p{IsHan}
- \p{IsHangul}
- \p{IsHanunoo}
- \p{IsHebrew}
- \p{IsHiragana}
- \p{IsInherited}
- \p{IsKannada}
- \p{IsKatakana}
- \p{IsKhmer}
- \p{IsLao}
- \p{IsLatin}
- \p{IsLimbu}
- \p{IsMalayalam}
- \p{IsMongolian}
- \p{IsMyanmar}
- \p{IsOgham}
- \p{IsOriya}
- \p{IsRunic}
- \p{IsSinhala}
- \p{IsSyriac}
- \p{IsTagalog}
- \p{IsTagbanwa}
- \p{IsTaiLe}
- \p{IsTamil}

- \p{IsTelugu}
- \p{IsThaana}
- \p{IsThai}
- \p{IsTibetan}
- \p{IsYi}

Unicode blocks: Java supports all the previously listed script for matching Unicode blocks. We just need to replace Is with In in the preceding expressions. For example, to check for a **Thai** code block, we can use:

```
\p{InThai}
```

Examples of matching Unicode text in regular expressions

The following regex will match accented characters, such as "à":

```
^\p{L}+$
```

The following regex will match a text consisting of Latin characters and Unicode whitespaces:

```
^[\p{IsLatin}\p{Zs}]+$
```

The following regex should be used to detect the presence of a **Hebrew** character in input:

```
\p{InHebrew}
```

The following regex should be used to detect an input that contains only **Arabic** text:

```
^\p{InArabic}+$
```

How can we match Urdu text? Since Urdu is not a script, we will need to match certain Unicode code ranges. These are as follows:

```
U+0600 to U+06FF
U+0750 to U+077F
U+FB50 to U+FDFF
U+FE70 to U+FEFF
```

A Java regex to detect the presence of any Urdu character will be:

```
[\u0600-\u06FF\u0750-\u077F\uFB50-\uFDFF\uFE70 -\uFEFF]
```

Double escaping in a Java String when defining regular expressions

In Java, all the regular expressions are entered as a String type, where \ acts as an escape character and is used to interpret certain special characters such as \t, \n, and so on. So, it is necessary to double-escape all the predefined classes, such as \w, \d, \s, using two backslashes and while escaping metacharacters, such as \ [, \ (, \+, and so on, in string literals.

If we have to use the preceding regex for a dollar amount in Java, then it would be as follows:

```
final String re = "\\$\\d+\\.\\d+";
```

The preceding example that matches a signed decimal number has to be written as follows in Java:

```
final String re = "^[+-]?\\d*\\.?\\d+$";
```

For the same reasons, if we have to match a single backslash character, then it would be as follows:

```
\\\\
```

How can we write a regex string that matches an input that allows any alphanumeric character, hyphen, dot, or backslash, such as xyzTR-4.5\00? Here is how:

```
final String re = "^[a-zA-Z0-9.\-\\\\]+$";
```

How can we write a regular expression in Java that will accept any Latin character, Unicode whitespaces, or Unicode digits? Refer to the following regex:

```
final String re = "^[\\p{IsLatin}\\p{Zs}\\p{N}]+$";
```

How to write a regular expression in Java that will accept any Unicde character, Unicode whitespaces, Unicode digits, or Unicode punctuation characters? Check out the following regex:

```
final String re = "^[\\p{L}\\p{Z}\\p{N}\\p{P}]+$";
```

The following Java regex matches the string, **abc:][}{**:

```
final String re = "abc:\\]\\[\\}\\{";
```

Embedded regular expression mode modifiers

Like all other regular expression flavors, Java also allows the **embedding** of some standard modes in the regular expression itself. These mode modifiers are used to change regular expression behavior in a certain manner. In the following table, we will list all these modes and their meaning:

Mode	Name	Meaning
(?i)	Ignore case mode	Enables case-insensitive matching for US-ASCII text
(?s)	DOTALL mode	Makes DOT match all the characters, including line breaks
(?m)	Multiline mode	Makes the carrot and dollar match the start and end of each line in a multiline input
(?u)	Unicode-aware case folding	Enables Unicode-aware case folding
(?U)	Unicode matching	Enables the Unicode version of predefined character classes and POSIX character classes.
(?d)	Unix line mode	Enables Unix lines mode
(?x)	Comment mode	Allows for the presence of whitespace and comments in the regex pattern

Let's check some examples to understand these modes better.

How to match an input in which the starting word is **Java** and the ending word is **Mode**, and we don't know what is in between these two words? Also, the input may contain line breaks as well.

Consider the following example input text, which is in two lines:

```
Java regex
Embedded Mode
```

Let's use the following regex:

```
\AJava.*Mode\z
```

If we use the preceding regex, then the match will fail because we know that DOT matches all the characters except line breaks by default. Hence, we need to enable the DOTALL mode here using the following:

```
(?s)\AJava.*Mode\z
```

Our regex will match the input because `(?s)` will enable the **DOTALL** mode and then `.*` will match the text between **Java** and **Mode**.

It is considered good practice to insert comments and line breaks in a complex and lengthy regular expression. In order to allow that, we will need to enable the comment mode using `(?x)`.

Here is an example of a regex with comments and extra whitespaces using multiple modifiers, including `(?x)`:

```
String regex = "(?ixs)\\A # assert start of the string\n"
    + "java\n"
    + "\\s\n"
    + "regex\n"
    + ".* # match 0 or more of any character including line breaks\n"
    + "Mode\n"
    + "\\z # assert end of the string";
```

It is interesting to note that this regular expression will still match the input text that we used in the previous example. You can clearly see how the use of `(?x)` allows us to use arbitrary white-spaces and inline comments in our regex.

Let's examine the use of the **MULTILINE** mode. In the same input text, that is, `Java regex\nEmbedded Mode`, what would be the regular expression that validates the first line only, which contains the text, *Java regex*?

Let's use anchors (caret and dollar) and write the regex as follows:

```
^Java regex$
```

This regex will **fail** to match our input because the input contains two lines and `$` will not assert the position at the end of every line without enabling the **MULTILINE** mode.

Change your regex to the following:

```
(?m)^Java regex$
```

And bingo! Our regex works now because we enabled the **MULTILINE** mode using `(?m)` at the start of the regex.

The placement of embedded modes in a Java regular expression

All the aforementioned embedded modes can be placed at the start of a regular expression to enable one or more modes for the complete regular expression. We can also place these modes in the middle of a regex to enable it for a specific group or a remainder of the regex pattern.

We can also **combine** multiple mode modifiers into a single expression like this:

```
(?is)
```

This enables the DOTALL and ignore case modes.

Disabling mode modifiers

To disable a previously enabled mode, we can place a hyphen (–) before the modifier symbol anywhere in your regular expression.

Let's look at some examples.

To disable DOTALL, we can use the following regex:

```
(?-s)
```

To disable ignore case matching, we can use the following regex:

```
(?-i)
```

To disable the MULTILINE mode, we can use the following regex:

```
(?-m)
```

To disable both ignore case and MULTILINE mode, we can use the following regex:

```
(?-im)
```

To disable the ignore case, DOTALL, and MULTILINE modes, we can use the following regex:

```
(?-ism)
```

Summary

In this chapter, we covered the core constructs of regular expressions in depth. You learned anchors, quantifiers, boundary matchers, various character classes, negated character classes, and predefined character classes. We found out that escaped characters need to be escaped twice in the Java language. You also learned Unicode text matching using regular expressions in Java. We covered greedy, non-greedy, and possessive quantifiers. You learned embedded mode modifiers in Java regular expressions and how they can change the interpretation of a regular expression.

In the next chapter, we will cover another very important feature of regular expressions, called grouping. You will learn the various types of grouping available in Java regular expressions and how to use them.

3
Working with Groups, Capturing, and References

In this chapter, you will learn how to match, capture, and reference substrings from a given input text using regular expressions. We will cover various types of groups available in Java, and the naming and numbering of captured groups. Readers will also learn how to use back reference or forward reference of the capturing groups.

We will be covering the following topics in this chapter:

- Grouping
- Capturing groups
- Group numbering
- Non-capturing groups
- Back references
- Named groups
- Forward references
- Invalid references

Capturing groups

Groups are a very useful feature of regular expressions, which are supported in all the flavors of regular expressions. Groups are used to combine multiple characters or multiple smaller components of regular expressions into a single unit. We create groups by placing a series of characters or subpatterns inside round brackets or parentheses, (and). For example, consider the following regex pattern:

```
(blue|red)
```

It means a capturing group that uses alternation. It either matches the letters b, l, u, and e or it matches the letters r, e, and d. In other words, it matches the strings blue or red, and more importantly, it creates a capturing group with either of the two matched strings. Each group becomes a single unit that can be used to apply certain constructs to the entire group. For example, anchors, boundary assertion, quantifiers, or alternation can be restricted to a part of the regular expression represented by the group. For example, look at the following regex pattern:

```
^Regular(Expression)?$
```

This regular expression will match the string, Regular, at the start. After that, there is one capturing group with the string, Expression; however, due to the placement of the ? quantifier after the group, it will match the 0 or 1 occurrence of the preceding group, making it an **optional capturing group**. Hence, this regex will either match the string, Regular, with an **empty** first capturing group or it will match the string RegularExpression, with the substring, Expression, in the first capturing group.

If we are given a problem to write a regular expression that matches only an even number of digits in the input, then we can use this pattern:

```
^([0-9]{2})+$
```

Since the + quantifier (one or more) is used next to the group that matches a pair of digits, this quantifier is applied to the entire group. Hence, this regular expression will match one or more pairs of digits (2, 4, 6, 8, 10, ...), or in simple words, it matches an even number of digits.

A regular expression can have multiple capturing groups, which can be nested inside each other as well.

For example, in the following regular expression, there are three capturing groups:

```
^((\d+)-([a-zA-Z]+))$
```

The preceding expression will match the input string, that is, `1234-aBc` with the following groups:

1. Group 1: `1234-aBc`
2. Group 2: `1234`
3. Group 3: `aBc`

Group numbering

Capturing groups are numbered in increasing numbers, starting with number one. Java regular expressions support up to 99 capturing groups. Group zero always stands for the entire matched text.

For nested capturing groups, group numbers are incremented with the appearance of the opening parenthesis from left to right.

To understand this better, let's consider the following regular expression with nested multiple capturing groups:

```
(((a|b)-(c|d))/(\d+))
```

It will match the input string as follows:

```
a-c/15
a-d/99
b-c/567
b-d/1000
```

For the input string, `a-c/15`, we will get the following captured groups:

Group Num	Captured Text
Group 0	`a-c/15`
Group 1	`a-c/15`
Group 2	`a-c`
Group 3	`a`
Group 4	`c`
Group 5	`15`

Also note that in the case of repeated matches in a capturing group using a quantifier, it will capture the last matched text in the given group.

For example, consider the following regex:

```
(\w+\s+){3}
```

If the input text is `around the word`, then the captured group number one will contain `word` after the regex execution, even though it also matches `around` and `the` before completing the match with the last word.

Named groups

In Java regular expressions, capturing groups can be defined in two ways:

1. Using numbers that get incremented automatically (as we discussed earlier).
2. Using names.

Starting from Java 7, the regular expressions API offers support for named capturing groups. Named capturing groups are especially useful where there are lots of capturing groups. If we have to insert a new group or remove an existing group, then the numerical order changes for every capturing group that comes after the new or removed group, thus requiring the updating of all those references.

The syntax for defining a capturing group is as follows:

```
(?<name>RE)
```

In the preceding line, RE is the pattern we are using for capturing a group.

There are certain rules to specify a named group in Java:

1. Names are case sensitive, so these are four different named capturing groups:
   - `(?<name>RE)`
   - `(?<Name>RE)`
   - `(?<NAME>RE)`
   - `(?<naME>RE)`

2. A name must satisfy the following regular expression:

   ```
   [a-zA-Z][a-zA-Z0-9]*
   ```

This means that the name must start with a letter and may contain letters or digits after the first position.

3. Names cannot be duplicate in Java regex.

Keep in mind that even when we use a name to define groups, the groups are still numbered as \1, \2, \3, and so on, and that these numbers can also be used in references.

For example, in the following regular expression, we are specifying four named groups, id, subject, score, and term, all separated by a colon:

```
(?<id>\d+):(?<subject>[a-zA-Z]+):(?<score>\d+):(?<term>[A-Z]+)
```

If matched with 123456:Science:97:II, then the following groups will be captured:

```
Group "id": "123456"
Group "subject": "Science"
Group "score": "97"
Group "term": "II"
Group 1: "123456"
Group 2: "Science"
Group 3: "97"
Group 4: "II"
```

Non-capturing groups

There are cases while building regular expressions when we don't really want to capture any text but just want to group a subpattern to apply a boundary assertion or quantifier. This is the case for using non-capturing groups. We can mark a group as a non-capturing group by *adding a question mark and a colon* right after the opening parenthesis.

Note that we can also place one or more mode modifiers between the question mark and the colon. The scope of the modifier used in this manner is only effective for that group.

For example, we can use a non-capturing group in our regex to match an even number of digits:

```
^(?:\d{2})+$
```

Since we are not really interested in capturing any text from a matched string, it is a good choice to use a non-capturing group here.

An example of a non-capturing group with the ignore case modifier is as follows:

```
(?i:red|green|blue|white)
```

Due to the presence of the i modifier, this capturing group will match all the alternations by ignoring the case. Thus, it may match red, RED, White, blue, Green, BluE, greeN, WHITE, and so on.

There are major differences between the following three regular expression patterns:

```
(?:abc)
(?mi:abc)
((?:abc)?)
```

In the first case, we define a non-capturing group with a pattern as abc.

In the second case, we define a non-capturing group with the m (*multiline*) and i (*ignore case*) modifiers. This allows the regex to match abc, ABC, Abc, or aBC.

In the third case, we define an optional non-capturing group inside the capturing group that matches abc or an empty string in the captured group.

Advantages of non-capturing groups

A non-capturing group lets us use the grouping inside a regular expression without changing the numbers assigned to the back references (explained in the next section). This can be very useful in building large and complex regular expressions.

Non-capturing groups also give us the flexibility to add or remove groups from a long regular expression with multiple groups. If we have to insert a new group or remove an existing group, then the numerical order changes for every group on the right-hand side of the new or removed group.

Using a non-capturing group instead of a capturing group saves memory, as the regular expression engine doesn't need to store groups in buffers, thus optimizing the overall regex execution. It is recommended to mark each group as non-capturing when we do not want to extract a grouped substring or refer to them anywhere in the regular expression.

Back references

Back references provide a convenient way of matching a repeated character or repeated tokens in the input text. By using back references, the regular expression engine can match the **exact same text** as previously matched by a capturing group.

The syntax of a back reference is a backslash followed by a capturing group number, as shown in the following example:

```
\3
```

The preceding example is a back reference of the third capturing group.

In Java regular expressions, there can be up to 99 back references, each number referencing a captured group number.

For example, if we need to match a two-digit number with the restriction that both digits must be the same, then we need to capture the first digit and then use a back reference for the first captured group, as follows:

```
^(\d)\1$
```

Now, this regex will match any of these strings: 11, 22, 55, and 88.

We can also use quantifiers after back references as we use them with capturing or non-capturing groups.

For example, if we have to match a five-digit number with all the same digits, then we can use the following regex:

```
^(\d)\1{4}$
```

As an example, we want to create a regex that matches four pairs of digits, separated by the colon (:), dash (–), or slash (/) characters. We also require the digit pairs to be the same on the first and third positions, and likewise, they must also be the same on the second and fourth positions. For example, 12-45:12-45 and 56/00:56-00 will be a matching string, but 57-13-58:13 will not, because 57 in the first pair of digits is not the same as 58, which is the third pair of digits. We can write our regex as follows:

```
^(\d{2})[:/-](\d{2})[:/-]\1[:/-]\2$
```

Let's look at some more useful regular expressions using capturing groups and back references. Suppose we need to write a regular expression for two repeated words, separated by one or more non-word characters in between. We can write our regular expression as follows:

```
^(\w+)\W+\1$
```

The back reference, \1, will make sure we match the exact same word as matched by the first capturing group in this regular expression.

Next, we need to write a regular expression for quoted words. Words can be wrapped using single quotes or double quotes, but the mixing of quotes is not allowed. We can then write our regex as follows:

```
^(['"])\w+\1$
```

Here, this regex pattern matches and captures the opening single or double quote using a character class. On the other side of the word, we use the \1 back reference to ensure that the same quote is matched in the end.

Back references cannot be used inside a character class, as we learned earlier. There is no grouping inside a character class, and most of the special meta characters become just literals inside a character class.

Back reference of a named group

The syntax for the back reference of a named group is as follows:

```
\k<group1>
```

Here, group1 is the name of the named capturing group.

For example, we can write our regular expression of repeating numbers, using a named group and named back reference, as follows:

```
^(?<matchedDigits>\d+)\s+\k<matchedDigits>$
```

Here, we are defining a captured group called num to capture a number using the first, and then, we are using a back reference of the named group using \k<num>.

This will match inputs such as 1234 1234 or 989 989.

Since the named capturing groups are numbered automatically as well, we can write the same regular expression as follows:

```
^(?<num>\d+)\s+\1$
```

Replacement reference of a named group

We haven't yet discussed the Java API for regular expression replacement, but just for reference, it will be pertinent to discuss the syntax of a named group reference in a replacement string:

- `${group1}`: This will be replaced in the resulting string by the matched content of the named captured group, `group1`
- `$1`: This will be replaced in the resulting string by the matched content of the captured group number `1`

Note that the double escaping of String while defining a Java regular expression should be applied here in defining named groups, named back references, and numbered back references. Thus, repeating the previous regular expressions used in Java code:

```
final String regex = "^(?<num>\\d+)\\s+\\k<num>$";
```

or using numbered back references:

```
final String regex = "^(\\d+)\\s+\\1$";
```

Forward references

Back reference is the term used when a capturing group is referenced after we capture it. Likewise, a forward reference is the term for referencing a group before capturing the text using a captured group. In other words, the forward reference refers to a capturing group that appears later in the regular expression pattern. Forward references are only useful if we use them inside a repeated group, since the regex engine will be able to resolve captured groups and populate the forward reference while repeating a match using quantifiers.

As with most modern languages, Java allows us to use the forward reference of the captured group. Forward reference is a fairly complex concept to understand in regex.

Let's consider an example regex to understand better:

```
^(\d+)-(?:\2[\dA-Fa-f]{4}|(\d*\.?\d+:))+$
```

Here, in this pattern, you can see that we are using the group reference, \2, before defining the captured group number, 2, which comes later in the regex pattern as: (\d*\.?\d+:). For this reason, \2 is a forward reference instead of a backward reference.

With the preceding regex, the following string matches:

    666-6.6:6.6:abcd3.3:

The string matches because in the first repetition of the non-captured group, the second captured group becomes 6.6: and this can be referenced later.

The following string also matches because the second captured group is overwritten each time it is matched:

    666-3.3:5.5:5.5:abcd

The first value that the second captured group captures is 3.3:, but it is overwritten by 5.5: later, and this is matched the third time when the first part of the alternatives matches in the non-capturing group.

The following string, however, does not match, although the first capture of the second group will be the string, 3.3:, by the time it is required by the forward reference:

    666-3.3:abcd3.3:

Thus, as it is undefined, it does not match anything, not even the empty string. Therefore, the first part of the alternative group does not match, and at this point, the second half also does not match, thereby leading to a failed matching. This way, the captured group, in this case, never captures the string, 3.3:.

To summarize this behavior, the forward reference does reference something that is defined in the regular expression later, but only when the expression has already been matched at least once.

For this reason, there is no point in using a forward reference outside some repeated construct as a part of one member of an alternative matching.

Similarly, in the following example, the regex pattern uses a forward reference:

    ^(?:\1#color|(red|blue|white))+$

This anchored regex uses the **forward reference**, \1, before matching the literal text, #color, on the left-hand side of the alternation. On the right-hand side of the alternation, it matches one of the given colors and captures it in the first capturing group. The entire alternation has the + quantifier after to make repeated matches.

In the first attempt, \1 fails the match and forces the regex engine to attempt the right-hand side of the alternation and match a color to populate \1 with the matching color. If there is any text left to be matched in the input, the regex engine, in the second attempt, matches the now populated reference, \1, followed by #color as the first alternation or an allowed color as the second alternation. This process is repeated until the regex engine either matches the complete string or fails the match.

This will match any of the following strings:

```
blue
redblue
blueblueblue
redbluewhite
redred#color
whitewhite#color
blueredred#color
```

However, it won't match the following strings:

```
#color
red#color
bluered#color
redbluefruit
redbluered#color
```

Invalid (non-existing) backward or forward references

The Java regular expression engine handles back references to non-existing groups in the same manner as back references to existing groups. Invalid or non-existing back references do not participate in the match. This means that a regular expression with an invalid back reference always fails, although it does not cause any exception.

For example, consider the following regex example:

```
(apple|orange|banana)\2
```

The \2 back reference will be invalid because there is only one capturing group in this regular expression. Hence, the back reference of \2 always makes it a failed match against any input.

The same happens even when we have a regex pattern as follows:

```
\1
```

Due to a similar rule, it will fail to match an empty string as well.

Summary

In this chapter, you learned how to capture and reference substrings from an input text using regular expressions. Using non-capturing groups, we discussed how to optimize our regex patterns. We discussed the various types of groups available in Java regular expressions, the numbering of captured groups, and named groups. You also learned how to use back reference and forward reference of the capturing groups using numbered and named references. In the next chapter, you will get to writing code in Java to evaluate regular expressions. You will also be introduced to Java regular expressions using the Java String API, and then, we will move on to regex capabilities in the Java Scanner API.

4

Regular Expression Programming Using Java String and Scanner APIs

In this chapter, you will be introduced to Java regular expressions using Java String methods and we will move on to regular expression capabilities in Java Scanner API.

We will cover the following topics in this chapter:

- Java String methods that use regular expressions
- What these methods are used for and how to use them
- The use of regular expressions in Java Scanner

So far, we have covered many theoretical concepts of writing regular expressions in depth. The time has now come to see some of these regular expressions in action. We are going to introduce you to Java programs evaluating these regular expressions using the `java.lang.String` and `java.util.Scanner` APIs.

Introduction to the Java String API for regular expressions' evaluation

The Java String API provides some useful methods to evaluate regular expressions against a text represented by the `String` object. Let's list those methods from the `String` class:

Method Signature	Purpose
boolean matches(String regex)	Matches the given regular expression against the string that the method is invoked on and returns true/false, indicating whether the match is successful (true) or not (false).
String `replaceAll`(String regex, String replacement)	Replaces each substring of the subject string that matches the given regular expression with the replacement string and returns the new string with the replaced content.
String `replaceFirst`(String regex, String replacement)	This method does the same as the previous one with the exception that it replaces only the first substring of the subject string that matches the given regular expression with the replacement string and returns the new string with the replaced content.
`String[]` split(String regex)	Splits the subject string using the given regular expression into an array of substrings (example given ahead).
`String[]` split(String regex, int limit)	This overloaded method does the same as the previous one but there is an additional second parameter. The `limit` parameter controls the number of times regular expressions are applied for splitting.

For the complete reference of the String class, refer to `https://docs.oracle.com/javase/8/docs/api/java/lang/String.html`.

Method - boolean matches(String regex)

This method attempts to match a given regular expression against the complete subject String and returns **true/false**, indicating whether the match is successful or not. The following are a few important points to note:

- Regular expression is applied against the entire String; there is no partial matching
- Regular expression does not need to be anchored using ^ and $, since it is matched against the entire input
- The equivalent of `Pattern.matches`(**String regex**, `CharSequence`**input**) method (will be covered later)

Example of the matches method

Let's look at a few examples to understand this method better.

The following code snippet using the `matches` method will return false:

```
"1234".matches("\\d");
```

It is because the `matches` method attempts to apply a given regex against the entire input and effectively runs this code as:

```
"1234".matches("^\\d$");
```

This will obviously fail as we have three digits in the input, not just one.

The code that matches the string "1234" and the call to the `matches()` method that returns `true` will use the quantifier + or * after `\\d`. Therefore, the following two method calls will return `true`:

```
"1234".matches("\\d+");
"1234".matches("\\d+");
```

To validate a given string that contains the colors **red, blue,** or **green**, we shall use this code listing:

```
package example.regex;

public class StringMatches
{
  public static void main(String[] args)
  {
```

```
        boolean result;
        String regex;
        String input = "Sky is blue";          // First regex
        regex = "\\b(red|blue|green)\\b";
        result = input.matches(regex);
        System.out.printf("Match result: %s%n", result);
        // prints false

        // Second regex
        regex = ".*\\b(red|blue|green)\\b.*";
        result = input.matches(regex);
        System.out.printf("Match result: %s%n", result);
        // prints true
    }
}
```

A few points about this regex are as follows:

- Alternation (**red** | **blue** | **green**) is being used to match any of the allowed colors
- The first regex fails to match because we are only matching the allowed colors using alternation but are not matching the text on either side of the alternation
- The second regex succeeds as we are using . * on both sides of the alternation to match any text before and after the allowed colors in the input text
- We are also using the word, **boundary assertions**, around our alternation expression to ensure that we match complete words only

To verify that the given input starts and ends with an English letter while allowing digits, letters, underscores, and hyphens in the middle, we can use the following regular expression in the `matches()` method:

```
input.matches("[a-zA-Z][a-zA-Z0-9_-]*[a-zA-Z]");
```

Else, we can also use the predefined class, \w:

```
input.matches("[a-zA-Z][\w-]*[a-zA-Z]");
```

In addition, we can use the modifier, (?i):

```
input.matches("(?i)[a-z][\w-]*[a-z]");
```

To verify that the input contains six to nine digits, use the following:

```
input.matches("\\d{6,9}");
```

Method - String replaceAll(String regex, String replacement)

This method replaces each substring of the subject string that matches the given regular expression with the replacement String. As the name implies, `replaceAll` replaces all the matching occurrences of the input String. Note that we can also supply a simple String containing no regex meta character in the first argument.

Calling this method is equivalent to a call to the following:

```
Pattern.compile(regex).matcher(input).replaceAll(replacement);
```

 Note: We will cover Pattern and Matcher APIs in `Chapter 5`, *Introduction to Java Regular Expression APIs - Pattern and Matcher Classes*.

The replacement string allows the use of references to substrings, represented by the captured groups used in the regular expression. These references can be of two types:

- **Numbered references**: These are written as `$n`, where n is a number, such as `$1`, `$2`, and `$3`, which represent a reference to each of the captured groups in the regular expression
- **Named references**: These are written as `${groupName}`, where `groupName` is the name of the captured group in the regular expression

To place a literal dollar or literal backslash in the replacement string, we need to escape these characters using double backslash (\\).

Here, at this point, you should understand the difference between back-reference and replacement reference. Back-reference is used in the regular expression pattern itself and is written as **\1**, **\2**, **\3**, and so on for a numbered group's back-reference and **\k<groupName>** for a named group's back-reference. However, replacement reference is either written as **$1, $2, $3**, for a numbered group's reference or **${groupName}** for a named group's reference.

Examples of the replaceAll method

To replace all the semi-colons with hyphens, we can use the following:

```
input = input.replaceAll(";", "-");
```

To remove all the non-digits from the input, we can use:

```
input = input.replace("\\D+", "");
```

To replace all the leading and trailing commas from an input, we can use an alternation regex:

```
input = input.replaceAll("^,+|,+$", "");
```

To replace all the occurrences of two or more white spaces with a single space, we can use:

```
input = input.replaceAll("\\s{2,}", " ");
```

How can we escape all the dollar signs that are just before the % character? In other words, to replace all the occurrences of $% with \$%, we can use:

```
input = input.replaceAll("\\$%", "\\\\\\$%");
```

Note that we are using \\\\ (four backslashes) to enter a single \, and we're using \\$ to enter a single $ in the replacement, whereas % will just be a literal.

Consider the following input:

```
$200 $%apple% $%banana% $%orange%
```

It will be converted into this:

```
$200 \$%apple% \$%banana} \${orange}
```

We can also leverage the group reference $0 here, which is populated with the entire matched text using a regex. So, our code can be simplified to this as $0 will refer to the matched text $% by our regex:

```
input = input.replaceAll("\\$%", "\\\\$0");
```

Another nice trick we can use here is to use the static method, `Matcher.quoteReplacement` that is in the `Matcher` API. This method handles all the special characters in a replacement string and escapes them appropriately. Now, our code can become this:

```
input = input.replaceAll("\\$%", Matcher.quoteReplacement("\\") + "$0");
```

Let's solve an interesting problem. We need to replace all the multiple occurrences of non-word characters with a single instance of the same character.

Consider the following input text:

```
Let''''''s learn::: how to    write cool regex...
```

The expected output is:

```
Let's learn: how to write cool regex.
```

Note that we are replacing multiple occurrences of non-word characters only and not replacing multiple occurrences of word characters.

Here is the code listing to solve this problem:

```
package example.regex;

public class StringReplaceAll
{
  public static void main(String[] args)
  {
    // our input string
    String input = "Let''''''s learn::: how to    write cool regex...";

    // call replaceAll and assign replaced string to same variable
    input = input.replaceAll("(\\W)\\1+", "$1");

    // print the result
    System.out.printf("Replaced result: %s%n", input);
  }
}
```

Here are a few points about this solution:

- We are using the predefined class, `\W`, to match a non-word character
- We are using a capturing group around the non-word character to be able to use a back-reference later in the regex and in the replacement

- The pattern, (\\W)\\1+, is used to match two or more occurrences of the same non-word character
- \1 represents the back-reference to the first captured group
- In the replacement, we are using the reference, $1, to place the captured non-word character back in the replaced string
- $1 represents the reference to the first captured group
- Using the named group directives that you learnt in the previous chapter, we can also write the replaceAll method call as follows:

```
input = input.replaceAll("(?<nwchar>\\W)\\k<nwchar>+", "${nwchar}");
```

Method - String replaceFirst(String regex, String replacement)

This method replaces the first substring of the subject string, which matches the given regular expression with the replacement String. As the name implies, replaceFirst replaces only the first matching occurrence of the input String. Note that we can also supply a simple String containing no regex meta character in the first argument as regex.

Calling this method is equivalent to the following call:

```
Pattern.compile(regex).matcher(input).replaceFirst(replacement);
```

 Note: We will cover the Pattern and Matcher APIs in later chapters.

A replacement string allows the use of group references, such as $1, $2, $3, and so on, for numbered references or ${groupName} for named references, which represent each of the captured groups in the regular expressions. To place a literal dollar or a literal backslash in the replacement, we need to escape these characters using the double backslash.

Examples of the replaceFirst method

To replace *only the first* semi-colon with a hyphen, we can use the following:

```
input = input.replaceFirst(";", "-");
```

What will be the output if we have to use the `replaceFirst` method instead of `replaceAll` in the input text of "`$%apple% $%banana% $%orange%`" for escaping the dollar signs?

The code will become as follows:

```
input = input.replaceFirst("\\$", "\\\\\\$");
```

It will replace only the first $ sign; hence, the output will only have the first $ escaped as follows:

```
\$%apple% $%banana% $%orange%
```

To replace the first dot of an IPV4 IP address with a colon, we can use the following code:

```
String newip = ipaddress.replaceFirst("\\.", ":");
```

Only the first dot will be replaced by a colon; hence, an IP value of `10.11.22.123` will become `10:11.22.123`.

Methods - String split methods

The String class has two split methods with the following signatures:

- String[] split(String regex, int limit)
- String[] split(String regex)

These split methods split the subject string into an array around the matches of the given regular expression, also called delimiters.

When there is a *positive width* match at the beginning of an input string, then an empty string is included at the beginning of the resulting array. However, a match of *zero width* by regular expression does not include any empty string at the beginning of the resulting array.

The array returned by this method contains a combination of the following elements:

- Token substrings that are split by the delimiter, matched using the given regular expression
- Input substring beyond the last match of the delimiter, using the given regular expression

- A leading empty string when there is a *positive width* delimiter
- Trailing empty strings (see the next subsection on the limit parameter)

When splitting regular a expression does not match any part of the input, the resulting array will just have a single element, that is, the complete input string.

`split(String regex)` is just an overloaded method with the same functionality that calls the two-argument split method with the limit parameter as zero, thus making a call as:

```
split(regex, 0)
```

The limit parameter rules

The limit parameter controls the number of times the regular expression pattern is applied for splitting the subject string. It affects the length of the resulting array with the following rules:

1. If the limit is greater than 0, then the pattern will be applied at most one time, the resulting array's length will not be greater than the limit, and the array's last entry will contain all input substrings beyond the last matched delimiter.
2. If the limit is negative, then the pattern will be applied as many times as possible, and the resulting array can have any length.
3. If the limit is zero (as in the single parameter split method call), then the pattern will be applied as many times as possible, the array can have any length, and **trailing empty strings will be discarded**.

Examples of the split method

Let's look at the following code listing, which splits the subject string on each occurrence of a hyphen:

```
package example.regex;

import java.util.*;

class StringSplit
{
  public static void main (String[] args)
  {
    final String input = "green-red-blue-yellow";

    Arrays.stream(input.split("-"))
```

```
        .forEach(System.out::println);
    }
}
```

This will generate the following output:

```
"green"
"red"
"blue"
"yellow"
```

Now, let's change our code to the following by splitting on each occurrence of the letter e:

```
Arrays.stream(input.split("e"))
.forEach(System.out::println);
```

The preceding code will generate the following output:

```
"gr"
""
"n-r"
"d-blu"
"-y"
"llow"
```

We got one empty result because we split on each e and there are two e letters in green, thus giving us an empty string between the two e letters.

Now, let's change our code to the following by splitting on one or more occurrences of e:

```
Arrays.stream(input.split("e+"))
.forEach(System.out::println);
```

We will get the following output:

```
"gr"
"n-r"
"d-blu"
"-y"
"llow"
```

We did not get any empty results now because we split on each e+ and the two e letters in green are matched in a single match.

Example of the split method using the limit parameter

To understand the impact of the `limit` parameter, let's take a comma-separated input string with two trailing commas:

```
fox,tiger,wolf,,
```

We can call the `split` method in two ways. We can call the `split` method with `limit=0`:

```
String[] arr = input.split(",", 0);
```

We can also call the single parameter `split` method call as:

```
String[] arr = input.split(",");
```

It splits the input string around a comma and the trailing empty strings are discarded, with the following values being returned by the `split` method:

```
"fox"
"tiger"
"wolf"
```

Now, let's call the `split` method with `limit=1`:

```
String[] arr = input.split(",", 1);
```

It splits the input string around a comma and then gets a single element in the resulting array, that is, the input string itself. The following value is returned by the `split` method:

```
"fox,tiger,wolf,,"
```

Let's call the `split` method with `limit=2`:

```
String[] arr = input.split(",", 2);
```

It splits the input string around a comma and then gets exactly two elements in the resulting array. The following two values are returned by the `split` method:

```
"fox"
"tiger,wolf,,"
```

Let's call the `split` method with `limit=3`:

```
String[] arr = input.split(",", 3);
```

It splits the input string around a comma, and then we get exactly three elements in the resulting array. The following three values are returned by the `split` method:

```
"fox"
"tiger"
"wolf,,"
```

Let's call the `split` method with a negative limit:

```
String[] arr = input.split(",", -1);
```

It splits the input string around a comma **as many times as possible, with the trailing empty strings included in the split array**, and we get these elements in the resulting array. The following values are returned by the `split` method. Note the two empty strings at the end of the split array:

```
"fox"
"tiger"
"wolf"
""
""
```

Using regular expressions in Java Scanner API

A scanner is a utility class used for parsing the input text and breaking the input into tokens of various types, such as Boolean, int, float, double, long, and so on. It generates tokens of various types using regular expression-based delimiters. The default delimiter is a whitespace. Using the Scanner API, we can generate tokens of all the primitive types in addition to string tokens.

The `String`, `Pattern`, and `Matcher` classes are able to parse the input and generate tokens of the `String` type only, but the `Scanner` class is very useful for checking and generating tokens of different types from the input source. The `Scanner` instance can be constructed using the `File`, `InputStream`, `Path`, `Readable`, `ReadableByteChannel`, and `String` arguments.

> `Pattern` and `Matcher` will be covered in detail in `Chapter 5`, *Introduction to Java Regular Expression APIs - Pattern and Matcher Classes*.

There are many methods in the scanner that support regular expressions. Let's list those methods down and understand them better:

Method Signature	Purpose
Scanner useDelimiter(String pattern)	Sets this scanner's delimiter regex pattern to a String regex argument.
Scanner useDelimiter(Pattern pattern)	This method is almost the same as the previous one but gets a `Pattern` as an argument instead of a `String`. This means that we can pass a regular expression already compiled. If we are forced to use the version with the `String` argument, the scanner would compile the string to a `Pattern` object even if we have already executed that compilation in other parts of the code. We will discuss the `Pattern` and `Matcher` class in the next chapter.
Pattern delimiter()	Returns the pattern being used by this scanner to match delimiters.
MatchResult match()	Returns the match result of the latest scan operation performed by this scanner.
boolean hasNext(String pattern)	Returns `true` if the next token matches the pattern constructed from the specified string.
boolean hasNext(Pattern pattern)	This method is almost the same as the previous one but gets `Pattern` as an argument instead of `String`.
String next(String pattern)	Returns the next token if it matches the pattern constructed from the specified string.
String next(Pattern pattern)	This method is almost the same as the previous one but gets `Pattern` as an argument instead of `String`.
String findInLine(String pattern)	Attempts to find the next occurrence of a pattern constructed from the specified string, ignoring delimiters.

String findInLine(Pattern pattern)	This method is almost the same as the previous one but gets `Pattern` as an argument instead of `String`.
Scanner skip(String pattern)	Skips the input that matches a pattern constructed from the specified string, ignoring delimiters.
Scanner skip(Pattern pattern)	This method is almost the same as the previous one but gets `Pattern` as an argument instead of `String`.
String findWithinHorizon(String pattern, int horizon)	Attempts to find the next occurrence of a pattern constructed from the specified string, ignoring delimiters.
String findWithinHorizon(Pattern pattern, int horizon)	This method is almost the same as the previous one but gets `Pattern` as an argument instead of `String`.

In addition to the two `hasNext()` methods mentioned in the preceding table using regular expression, the `Scanner` class also provides several overloaded `hasNext` methods that return `true` if the next available token in the input can be retrieved for that particular type. For example: `hasNextInt()`, `hasNextDouble()`, `hasNextBoolean()`, `hasNextByte()`, `hasNextFloat()`, `hasNextLong()`, `hasNextShort()`, `hasNextBigInteger()`, `hasNextBigDecimal()`, `hasNext()`.

Similarly, there are several overloaded `next` methods that scan the input to return the next token for that particular type. For example: `nextextInt()`, `nextextDouble()`, `nextextBoolean()`, `nextextByte()`, `nextextFloat()`, `nextextLong()`, `nextextShort()`, `nextextBigInteger()`, `nextextBigDecimal()`, `nextext()`.

For the complete reference of the `Scanner` class refer to https://docs.oracle.com/javase/8/docs/api/java/util/Scanner.html.

Suppose there is an input text delimited by two exclamation marks. The data is structured in the following sequence:

```
animal!!id!!weight
```

The animal name is a string, id is an integer number, and weight is a double number.

With this structure, here is an example input:

```
Tiger!!123!!221.2!!Fox!!581!!52.50
```

Given that there are two animals, here is how we can use the Scanner class to parse this input data in Java:

```
final String input = "Tiger!!123!!221.2!!Fox!!581!!52.50";
final int MAX_COUNT = 2;
String animal;
int id;
double weight;

Scanner scanner = new Scanner(input).useDelimiter("!!");

for (int i=0; i<MAX_COUNT; i++)
{
    animal = scanner.next();
    id = scanner.nextInt();
    weight = scanner.nextDouble();

    System.out.printf("animal=[%s], id=[%d], weight=[%.2f]%n", animal,
id, weight);
}

scanner.close();
```

This is what is happening in this code:

- new Scanner(input) is the code to construct a scanner using the input string
- scanner.useDelimiter("!!") sets the delimiter regular expression as "!!"
- scanner.next() gets the next string token from the constructed scanner
- scanner.nextInt() gets the next int token from the scanner
- scanner.nextDouble() gets the next double token from the scanner
- scanner.close() closes the scanner object; we cannot generate further tokens from the scanner after this method call

As you can guess, we will get the following output from the preceding code:

```
animal=[Tiger], id=[123], weight=[221.20]
animal=[Fox], id=[581], weight=[52.50]
```

Let's parse a more complex input data to understand the use of the Scanner class better. Here is the complete code listing:

```
package example.regex;

import java.util.*;

public class ScannerApi
{
  public static void main (String[] args)
  {
    final String str = "London:Rome#Paris:1234:Munich///Moscow";

    Scanner scanner = new Scanner(str);

    scanner.useDelimiter("\\p{Punct}+");

    final String cityPattern = "\\p{L}+";

    while(scanner.hasNext()) {
      if(scanner.hasNext(cityPattern)) {
        System.out.println(scanner.next());
      }
      else {
        scanner.next();
      }
    }

    scanner.close();
  }
}
```

This is what is happening in this code:

- new Scanner(str) is the code to construct a scanner using the input string
- * scanner.useDelimiter("\\p{Punct}+") sets the delimiter regular expression as one or more punctuation characters
- We are using "\\p{L}+" as the acceptable city name pattern, which means one or more Unicode letters

- `scanner.hasNext(cityPattern)` returns `true` if the next token from the scanner matches `cityPattern`
- `scanner.next()` retrieves the next string token from the scanner
- `scanner.close()` closes the scanner object; we cannot generate further tokens from the scanner after this method call

Upon compiling and running the preceding code, it will produce the following output:

```
London
Rome
Paris
Munich
Moscow
```

Summary

In this chapter, you were introduced to Java programs using regular expressions using the String and Scanner classes. We discussed the methods available in these two APIs that are related to regular expression handling and how we can make use of those methods in our code.

In the next chapter, we will cover the Pattern and Matcher classes, which are the most important classes for programs using regular expressions.

5
Introduction to Java Regular Expression APIs - Pattern and Matcher Classes

In this chapter, we will introduce you to dedicated Java APIs for writing programs using regular expressions. Java provides a package, `java.util.regex`, which contains all the classes and interfaces for handling regular expressions. This package is in the `java.base` module, so we do not explicitly declare its use in the `module-info.java` source file. The `java.base` module is automatically required by all modules, and it contains the most important and basic JDK packages and classes. Regular expressions is such an important topic and tool that Java 9 experts decided to keep it inside the `java.base` module.

We will cover the following classes and interfaces from this package:

- The `MatchResult` interface
- Using `Pattern` class
- Using `Matcher` class
- Various methods of `Pattern` and `Matcher` classes and how to use them for solving problems involving regular expressions

The MatchResult interface

MatchResult is an interface for representing the result of a match operation. This interface is implemented by the Matcher class. This interface contains query methods used to determine the results of a match against a regular expression. The match boundaries, groups, and group boundaries can only be retrieved but not modified through this interface. Here is a list of important methods provided in this interface:

Method Name	Description
int start()	Returns the start index of the match in the input
int start(int group)	Returns the start index of the specified capturing group
int end()	Returns the offset after the last character matched
int end(int group)	Returns the offset after the last character of the subsequence captured by the given group during this match
String group()	Returns the input substring matched by the previous match
String group(int group)	Returns the input subsequence captured by the given group during the previous match operation
int groupCount()	Returns the number of capturing groups in this match result's pattern

Let's take an example to understand this interface better.

Suppose, the input string is a web server response line from HTTP response headers:

```
HTTP/1.1 302 Found
```

Our regex pattern to parse this line is as follows:

```
HTTP/1\.[01] (\d+) [a-zA-Z]+
```

Note that there is only one captured group that captures integer status code.

Let's look at this code listing to understand the various methods of the `MatchResult` interface better:

```java
package example.regex;

import java.util.regex.*;

public class MatchResultExample
{
  public static void main(String[] args)
  {
    final String re = "HTTP/1\\.[01] (\\d+) [a-zA-Z]+";
    final String str = "HTTP/1.1 302 Found";

    final Pattern p = Pattern.compile(re);
    Matcher m = p.matcher(str);

    if (m.matches())
    {
      MatchResult mr = m.toMatchResult();

      // print count of capturing groups
      System.out.println("groupCount(): " + mr.groupCount());

      // print complete matched text
      System.out.println("group(): " + mr.group());

      // print start position of matched text
      System.out.println("start(): " + mr.start());

      // print end position of matched text
      System.out.println("end(): " + mr.end());

      // print 1st captured group
      System.out.println("group(1): " + mr.group(1));

      // print 1st captured group's start position
      System.out.println("start(1): " + mr.start(1));

      // print 1st captured group's end position
      System.out.println("end(1): " + mr.end(1));
    }
  }
}
```

We retrieve a `MatchResult` instance after calling the required `Pattern` and `Matcher` methods (discussed in the next section). After compiling and running the preceding code, we will get the following output, which shows the use of the various methods of this interface:

```
groupCount(): 1
group(): HTTP/1.1 302 Found
start(): 0
end(): 18
group(1): 302
start(1): 9
end(1): 12
```

The Pattern class

The `Pattern` class represents the compiled form of a string regular expression. So far, we have provided all the regular expressions as strings. Each String regular expression must be compiled into an instance of the `Pattern` class before the Java regex engine can execute it. An instance of the `Pattern` class is used to create a `Matcher` object to match input text against the regular expression.

Let's list down the important and useful methods from the `Pattern` class first:

Method Signature	Description
Static Pattern compile(String regex)	Compiles the given String regular expression into a `Pattern` instance.
Static Pattern compile(String regex, int flags)	Compiles the given String regular expression into a Pattern instance with the given flags. Flags can be one or more of DOTALL, MULTILINE, CASE_SENSITIVE, UNICODE_CHARACTER_CLASS and a few others. Check the Java Pattern API at http://download.java.net/java/jdk9/docs/api/java/util/regex/Pattern.html for all flags and their descriptions.
Matcher matcher(CharSequence input)	Creates a `matcher` instance to match the given input against this compiled pattern.
String quote(String str)	Returns a literal pattern string for the specified string. After quoting the String, regex meta characters or escape sequences in the input string will just be literals without any special meaning. `Pattern.quote` wraps the given string in \\Q and \\E escape constructs. These special escape constructs are used to make a wrapped string as a literal string, thus removing all the special meanings of regex meta and special characters.

Predicate<String> asPredicate () Predicate<String> asPredicate ()	Creates a `Predicate` of a string to match the input string.
Stream<String> splitAsStream(CharSequence input)	Splits the given input string using this pattern and creates a stream from the given input sequence around the matches of this pattern (added in Java 8).
String[] split(CharSequence input)	Splits the given input sequence around the matches of this pattern. It is the same as `String.split(String regex)`.
String[] split(CharSequence input, int limit)	Splits the given input sequence around the matches of this pattern. The limit parameter controls the number of times the pattern is applied and, therefore, affects the length of the resulting array. It is the same as `String.split(String regex, int limit)`.

The `Pattern` class has a static method that can be called to match a string against a regular expression. This is as follows:

```
boolean matches(String regex, CharSequence input)
```

It can be used instead of the following:

```
final Pattern p = Pattern.compile(regex);
Matcher m = p.matcher(input);
m.matches();
```

This is actually the JDK9 implementation of this method. Although it is simpler and shorter to call this method instead of three lines, it is recommended to use the methods `compile()`, `matcher()`, and `matches()` separately if we perform matching against the same regular expression many times. In such a case, we can invoke `compile()` only the first time and keep the compiled pattern and avoid recompilation each time the matching is performed.

Examples using the Pattern class

Let's look at a few examples to understand some of these methods.

To compile a regular expression for decimal numbers, we can use the following code snippet:

```
final String decimalPattern = "^[+-]?\\d*\\.?\\d+$";
Final Pattern pattern = Pattern.compile(decimalPattern);
```

The static method, `Pattern.compile`, compiles a string regex and returns a `Pattern` instance.

To match text between ## and ## that may include newlines as well, we can use the following compiled pattern:

```
final String re = "##.*?##";
Final Pattern pattern = Pattern.compile(re, Pattern.DOTALL);
```

Here, we are using two parameters: the `Pattern.compile` method and passing `DOTALL` as a flag in the second parameter, since we want to match the newline as well as using our lazy pattern `.*?`.

> Note the use of lazy pattern `.*?` instead of greedy `.*` so that we match the shortest match between ## and ##.

We can also write the preceding code snippet using the inline mode modifier, `(?s)`:

```
final String re = "(?s)##.*?##";
Final Pattern pattern = Pattern.compile(re);
```

If we want to match a string that contains a subsequence, +-*/., surrounded by one or more white spaces on both the sides, then we can use the following code:

```
package example.regex;

import java.util.*;
import java.util.regex.*;

class PatternQuoteExample
{
  public static void main (String[] args)
  {
    String input = "Math operators: +-*/.   ";
    boolean result;

    String quoted = Pattern.quote("+-*/.");
    System.out.println(quoted);

    // regex using standard escaping
    result = input.matches(".*\\s+\\+-\\*/\\.\\s+.*");

    System.out.println(result);

    // regex Using Pattern.quote around our search string
```

```
        result = input.matches(".*\\s+" + quoted + "\\s+.*");

        System.out.println(result);

        // regex Using \Q and \E around our search string
        result = input.matches(".*\\s+\\Q+-*/.\\E\\s+.*");

        System.out.println(result);

    }
}
```

After compiling and running this code, will quoted string as: `"\Q+-*/.\E"` and then print true for all the three cases as the call to matches succeeds all the times. However, an important difference is the use of `Pattern.quote` in the second case, which handles the quoting of special regex characters in the search string, such as +, *, .

Then, in the third case, we just wrap our search string using `\\Q` and `\\E`, which is the same as calling `Pattern.quote` with our search string.

To split an input text on two pipes or | |, we can use following code:

```
package example.regex;

import java.util.*;
import java.util.regex.*;

class PatternSplitExample
{
    public static void main (String[] args)
    {
        final String input = "value1||value2||value3";
        final Pattern p = Pattern.compile(Pattern.quote("||"));

        // call split and print each element from generated array
        // using stream API
        Arrays.stream(p.split(input))
        .forEach(System.out::println);
    }
}
```

Consider the following few points about this code:

- We call `Pattern.quote` to avoid escaping double pipe string
- We call `Pattern.compile` to compile our string regex and get back a compiled Pattern object
- We use a generated pattern instance to call the `split` method by supplying an input string that we want to operate on

Java 8 added a new method, `splitAsStream`, which returns a stream containing the substring from the given input sequence around the matches of this pattern. Using `splitAsStream`, we can simplify the preceding class as follows:

```
package example.regex;

import java.util.*;
import java.util.regex.*;

class PatternSplitStreamExample
{
  public static void main (String[] args) throws java.lang.Exception
  {
    final String input = "value1||value2||value3";
    final Pattern p = Pattern.compile(Pattern.quote("||"));

    // call splitAsStream and print each element from generated stream
    p.splitAsStream(input)
    .forEach(System.out::println);
  }
}
```

Note the use of the `splitAsStream` method instead of the `Arrays.stream()` static method in this class. Creating an array performs the whole split. When `Pattern` returns a stream, it can do the splitting only when it is needed. If we, for example, limit the stream to work up only the first 10 elements, then the splitting does not need to do the splitting for further elements.

It is true even if some of the implementations just do the splitting and return an array based stream from `splitAsStream()`. A different implementation of the JDK is free to use a better solution only if we use `splitAsStream()` but has no choice if we use `split()` and convert to stream afterward.

Filtering a list of tokens using the asPredicate() method

As noted in the preceding table, the `asPredicate()` method creates a predicate that can be used to match an input string. Let's look at an example code listing to understand this method better:

```java
package example.regex;

import java.util.List;
import java.util.stream.*;
import java.util.regex.*;

public class AsPredicateExample
{
  public static void main(String[] args)
  {
    final String[] monthsArr =
{"10", "0", "05", "09", "12", "15", "00", "-1", "100"};

    final Pattern validMonthPattern =
Pattern.compile("^(?:0?[1-9]|1[00-2])$");

    List<String> filteredMonths = Stream.of(monthsArr)
      .filter(validMonthPattern.asPredicate())
      .collect(Collectors.toList());

    System.out.println(filteredMonths);
  }
}
```

This code has a list of month numbers as an array of `String`. The valid months are between `1` and `12` with an optional `0` before the single-digit months.

We use the following regex pattern for a valid month number:

```
^(?:0?[1-9]|1[00-2])$
```

We use the return value of the `asPredicate()` method to filter the stream of string array containing all the input month values.

After compiling and running, the preceding code will print the following output, which is a filtered list from the original list containing all the valid month numbers:

```
[10, 05, 09, 12]
```

The Matcher class

An instance of the `Matcher` class performs various match operations on a character sequence by interpreting a compiled regular expression represented by an instance of Pattern. This is how we use this class to match a regex:

- We create a matcher instance from a pattern by invoking the pattern's matcher method that requires the input sequence as argument
- The instance of matcher is used to perform three types of match operations using these three methods, each returning a Boolean value (true indicates success):
  - matches
  - find
  - lookingAt

These methods perform the matching in the following manner:

- The `matches` method attempts to match the *complete input sequence* using the matcher's pattern
- The `find` method *searches* the input sequence for the next substring that matches the pattern
- The `lookingAt` method attempts to match the input sequence using the matcher's pattern *at the start position.*

Let's list down all the important methods from the `Matcher` class here:

Method Signature	Description
boolean find()	Using the matcher's pattern attempts to find the next matching substring of the input text.
boolean find(int start)	This is the same as the previous, except that the search starts at the `start` position.
boolean matches()	Attempts to match the complete input text..
boolean lookingAt()	Attempts to match the input text, starting at the beginning of the region. It does not need to match the complete input text.
String group()	Returns the complete input text matched by the previous match.

String group(int group)	Returns the input text captured by the specified group number during the previous match operation.
String group(String groupName)	Returns the input text captured by the given named group during the previous match operation.
int groupCount()	Returns the number of capturing groups in this matcher's pattern.
int start()	Returns the start index of the previous match operation.
int start(int group)	Returns the start position of the text captured by the given group number during the previous match operation.
int start(int groupName)	Returns the start position of the text captured by the given named group during the previous match operation.
int end()	Returns the end position of the previous match operation.
int end(int group)	Returns the end position of the text captured by the given group number during the previous match operation.
int end(int groupName)	Returns the end position of the text captured by the given named group during the previous match operation.
Matcher appendReplacement(StringBuffer buffer, String replacement)	Appends the given replacement text to the string buffer after the last character of the previous match in the string buffer.
StringBuffer appendTail(StringBuffer buffer)	This method reads characters from the input text, starting at the append position, and appends them to the given string buffer. It is intended to be invoked after one or more invocations of the `appendReplacement` method in order to copy the remainder of the input text to the buffer.

Static String quoteReplacement(String s)	Returns a literal replacement String for the specified String. It makes backslashes and dollar signs to be treated literally.
String replaceAll(String replacement)	Using the current matcher's pattern, it replaces all the matched substrings of the input text with the given replacement string.
String replaceFirst(String replacement)	Using the current matcher's pattern, it replaces the first matched substring of the input text with the given replacement string.
Matcher reset()	Resets this matcher object and initializes all the internal states.
Matcher reset(CharSequence input)	Resets this matcher object with a new input text and initializes all the internal states.
MatchResult toMatchResult()	Returns the match result of the matcher that represents state of the match. This method is usually called after one of the `find/matches/lookingAt` method calls.
Matcher usePattern(Pattern newPattern)	Updates the pattern used by this matcher to find new matches.

Examples using the Matcher class

The `Matcher` class represents the main regular expression engine in Java that provides all the functionality and features required to match regular expressions against input. Let's look at some important methods of this class with practical examples to understand their use.

Method Boolean lookingAt()

The `lookingAt()` method attempts to match the input against the pattern, starting from the *beginning* of the input but without requiring that the entire region be matched against the pattern. The following code demonstrates it:

```
package example.regex;

import java.util.regex.*;
```

```
class MatcherLookingatExample
{
  public static void main (String[] args)
  {

    final Pattern pattern1 = Pattern.compile("master[a-z]*");
    final Pattern pattern2 = Pattern.compile("master");
    final Pattern pattern3 = Pattern.compile("regular");

    String input = "mastering regular expressions";

    Matcher matcher = pattern1.matcher(input);
    System.out.printf("[%s] => [%s]: %s%n", input, matcher.pattern(),
    matcher.lookingAt());

    // update the matcher's pattern  with a new pattern
    matcher.usePattern(pattern2);
    System.out.printf("[%s] => [%s]: %s%n", input, matcher.pattern(),
    matcher.lookingAt());

    // update the matcher's pattern  with a new pattern
    matcher.usePattern(pattern3);
    System.out.printf("[%s] => [%s]: %s%n", input, matcher.pattern(),
    matcher.lookingAt());

  }
}
```

Upon compiling and running, the preceding code produces following output:

```
[mastering regular expressions] => [master[a-z]*]: true
[mastering regular expressions] => [master]: true
[mastering regular expressions] => [regular]: false
```

You can see that the `lookingAt()` method returns `true` only when we supply patterns that are at the starting of the input, such as `master[a-z]*` and `master`, but returns `false` when we supply a pattern that is in the middle, such as `regular`.

The matches() method

The `matches()` method attempts to match the entire region against the pattern and returns `true` only if the entire region matches against the pattern.

Let's look at the following code to understand the use of this method better:

```
package example.regex;

import java.util.regex.*;

class MatcherMatchesExample
{
  public static void main (String[] args)
  {

    final Pattern pattern1 = Pattern.compile("mastering");
    final Pattern pattern2 = Pattern.compile("mastering.*");
    final Pattern pattern3 = Pattern.compile("regular.*");

    String input = "mastering regular expressions";

    Matcher matcher = pattern1.matcher(input);
    System.out.printf("[%s] => [%s]: %s%n", input, matcher.pattern(),
    matcher.matches());

    // update the matcher ppattern  with a new pattern
    matcher.usePattern(pattern2);
    System.out.printf("[%s] => [%s]: %s%n", input, matcher.pattern(),
    matcher.matches());

    // update the matcher ppattern  with a new pattern
    matcher.usePattern(pattern3);
    System.out.printf("[%s] => [%s]: %s%n", input, matcher.pattern(),
    matcher.matches());

  }
}
```

This will give following output after running:

```
[mastering regula expressions] => [mastering]: false
[mastering regula expressions] => [mastering.*]: true
[mastering regula expressions] => [regular.*]: false
```

As you can see, we get true only when our pattern matches the entire region from the start to end, which is using this regex: mastering.*

The find() and find(int start) methods

These `find` methods attempt to find the next subsequence of the input sequence that matches the pattern. These methods return `true` only if a subsequence of the input matches this matcher's pattern. If multiple matches can be found in the text, then the `find()` method will find the first, and then for each subsequent call to `find()`, it will move to the next match.

An example code will make it clearer:

```
package example.regex;

import java.util.regex.*;

class MatcherFindExample
{
  public static void main (String[] args)
  {
    final String input = "some text <value1> anything <value2><value3>
    here";

    /* Part 1 */
    final Pattern pattern = Pattern.compile("<([^<>]*)>");

    Matcher matcher = pattern.matcher(input);

    while (matcher.find()) {
      System.out.printf("[%d] => [%s]%n",
      matcher.groupCount(), matcher.group(1));
    }

    /* Part 2 */
    // now use similar pattern but use a named group and reset the
    // matcher
    matcher.usePattern(Pattern.compile("<(?<name>[^<>]*)>"));
    matcher.reset();

    while (matcher.find()) {
      System.out.printf("[%d] => [%s]%n",

      matcher.groupCount(), matcher.group("name"));
    }
  }
}
```

This will output the following:

```
[1] => [value1]
[1] => [value2]
[1] => [value3]
[1] => [value1]
[1] => [value2]
[1] => [value3]
```

As you can see in the preceding code, we are extracting all the text that is inside the angular brackets using a negated character class, `[^<>]*`, inside a capturing group.

In `Part 1` of the code, we use regular captured group and `matcher.group(1)` to extract and print the subsequence captured in group number 1. The numbering of the groups starts each time we execute `find()` and the previous captures are wiped off. Even though it is in a loop, it is always `group(1)` in the example because for each iteration, there can be more than one group.

In `Part 2`, we use a named capturing group and an overloaded method call to `matcher.group("name")` to extract the subsequence captured by the given group name.

The appendReplacement(StringBuffer sb, String replacement) method

This method is intended to be used in a loop together with the `appendTail` and `find` methods. Once we get a match using the `find()` method, we can call the `appendReplacement()` method to operate on each match and replace the matched text. Finally, it appends the replaced text to `StringBuffer`. It reads characters from the input sequence, starting at the append position, and appends them to the given string buffer. It stops after reading the last character preceding the previous match, that is, the character at index `start() - 1`.

The replacement string may contain references to subsequences captured during the previous match. All the rules of replacement reference we `String.replaceAll` apply to this method also.

The `appendReplacement()` method keeps track of what has been copied into `StringBuffer`, so we can keep searching for matches using `find()` in a loop, until no more matches are found in the input text. There will be an example following the next section.

Java 9 has another overloaded signature of this method to start accepting `StringBuilder` instead of `StringBuffer` as the first parameter.

The appendTail(StringBuffer sb) method

This method reads characters from the input sequence, starting at the append position, and appends them to the given string buffer. It is intended to be invoked after one or more invocations of the `appendReplacement` method in order to copy the remainder of the input sequence.

Just like in the case of the `appendReplacement()` method, there is also an overloaded version of the `appendTail()` method that accepts `StringBuilder`, which is not synchronized, instead of `StringBuffer`, which is synchronized.

Example of the appendReplacement and appendTail methods

Let's look at a complete program to the understand use of these methods.

Consider the following input:

```
<n1=v1 n2=v2 n3=v3> n1=v1 n2=v2 abc=123 <v=pq id=abc> v=pq
```

We need to write code to swap each name-value pair enclosed in angular brackets, < and >, while leaving the name-value pairs outside the angular brackets unchanged. After running our code, it should produce the following output:

```
<v1=n1 v2=n2 v3=n3> n1=v1 n2=v2 abc=123 <pq=v abc=id> v=pq
```

To solve this problem, we have to first find each match enclosed in angular brackets using the `find` method in a loop. Inside the loop, we will have to replace each name-value pair using the `appendReplacement` method. Finally, outside the loop, we will use the `appendTail` method to append the remaining characters after our last match.

Here is the full code:

```java
package example.regex;

import java.util.regex.*;

class MatcherAppendExample
{
  public static void main (String[] args)
  {
    final String input = "<n1=v1 n2=v2 n3=v3> n1=v1 n2=v2 abc=
    123 <v=pq id=abc> v=pq";

    // pattern1 to find all matches between < and >
    final Pattern pattern = Pattern.compile("<[^>]+>");

    // pattern1 to find each name=value pair
    final Pattern pairPattern = Pattern.compile("(\\w+)=(\\w+)");

    Matcher enclosedPairs = pattern.matcher(input);

    StringBuilder sbuf = new StringBuilder();

    // call find in a loop and call appendReplacement for each match
    while (enclosedPairs.find())
    {
      Matcher pairMatcher = pairPattern.matcher(enclosedPairs.group());
      // replace name=value with value=name in each match
      enclosedPairs.appendReplacement(sbuf,
      pairMatcher.replaceAll("$2=$1"));
    }

    // appendTail to append remaining character to buffer
    enclosedPairs.appendTail(sbuf);

    System.out.println(sbuf);
  }
}
```

Upon compiling and running, the preceding code will produce the following output:

```
<v1=n1 v2=n2 v3=n3> n1=v1 n2=v2 abc=123 <pq=v abc=id> v=pq
```

As you can see, the final output has all the `name=value` pairs swapped inside the angular brackets.

Summary

In this chapter, you learned about the most important regular expression handling Java classes. The `Matcher` and `Pattern` classes are heavy and complex tools that can be used to get really far when it comes to string manipulation. We have seen an example of a compound task, transforming name-value pairs inside a string, enclosed between angular brackets. If you imagine how hard it would have been without regular expressions and these classes, then you realize the power you now have in your hand after this chapter; it is almost wizard-level.

In the next chapter, we will move on to advanced topics of regular expressions, such as zero-width assertions, using the `lookahead` and `lookbehind` assertions, atomic groups, and so on.

6
Exploring Zero-Width Assertions, Lookarounds, and Atomic Groups

You will learn about zero-width assertions in Java regular expressions. We will cover various zero-width assertions and their usage patterns. We will then move on to learn the important topic of lookahead and lookbehind assertions in Java regular expressions and how to use them to solve some important problems. We will also discuss the use of atomic groups in Java regular expressions.

We will cover the following topics in this chapter:

- Zero-width assertions
- Previous match boundary
- Atomic groups
- Lookahead assertions: positive and negative
- Lookbehind assertions: positive and negative
- Capturing text from overlapping matches
- Capturing groups inside lookahead and lookbehind groups
- Lookbehind limitations in Java regular expressions

Zero-width assertions

Zero-width or zero-length assertion in regular expressions means that there is a zero-length match that does not change the current position of the pointer in the input string. These assertions do not consume characters in the string but only assert whether a match is possible or not, giving us a binary true or false match result. Although many zero-width assertions are denoted inside parentheses, like groups, we will soon see that they do not capture any text. Zero-width assertions have no real meaning in back-references or in replacements.

 We have already discussed a few zero-width assertions in the previous chapters, such as anchors and boundary assertions.

The Java regular expression engine allows many predefined zero-width assertions, including the ones we have discussed already, such as start, end anchors, and word boundaries.

Predefined zero-width assertions

Zero-width Assertion	Description
\b	Asserts a word boundary
\B	Asserts anywhere except at a word boundary
^	Asserts position only at the beginning of a line
$	Asserts position only at the end of a line
\A	Asserts position only at the beginning of a string
\z	Asserts position only at the end of a string
\Z	Asserts position only at the end of a string or before the line break at the end of a string (if present)
\G	Asserts position at the end of the previous match or at the start of the string for the very first match

Regex defined zero-width assertions

Regex defined zero-width assertions use (and) and there is a ? after the opening (. There are two assertions: positive, denoted by the = character, and negative, denoted by the ! character. If the assertion is backward-looking then the ? character is followed by a < character. Thus, (?=...) is a positive lookahead assertion and (?<!...) is a negative lookbehind assertion.

(?=pattern)	The positive lookahead assertion ensures that the string matches the pattern after the current position. For example, abc(?=K) ensures that the characters "abc" in the checked strings are followed by the letter "K", but this check does not consume the character "K".
(?!pattern)	The negative lookahead assertion ensures that the string does not match the pattern after the current position. For example, abc(?!Z) ensures that the characters "abc" in the checked string are not followed by the letter "Z", but this check does not consume the character "Z".
(?<=pattern)	The positive lookbehind assertion ensures that the string matches the pattern before the current position. For example, (?<=P)abc ensures that the characters "abc" in the checked string are preceded by the letter "P", but this check does not consume the character "P".
(?<!pattern)	The negative lookbehind assertion ensures that the string does not match the pattern before the current position. For example, (?<!Q)abc ensures that the characters "abc" in the checked string are not preceded by the letter "Q", but this check does not consume the character "Q".

In the next section, we will look into more details of the \G boundary assertions, and then, you will learn about the lookahead and lookbehind assertions. However, before the lookarounds, we will discuss atomic groups, which are an important construct and topic to ease the understanding of the behavior of the lookahead and lookbehind assertions.

\G boundary assertion

\G is a zero-width assertion. It is also a boundary matcher that asserts positions at the end of the previous match or at the start of the string, such as the \A assertion for the very first match. The Java regex engine remembers the position of \G within the context of a Matcher instance. If Matcher is instantiated again or is reset, then the position of \G is also initialized to the start of the string.

For example, consider the following input:

```
,,,,,123,45,67
```

Consider that we need to replace every comma that occurs only at the start of the input with a hyphen so that we have the same number of hyphens as the number of commas at the start. Our final output should be the following:

```
-----123,45,67
```

We cannot just do `replaceAll` by matching each comma, since that will also replace the comma after `123` and `45`, and moreover, we want the same number of hyphens as the number of commas in the input string.

For cases like this, we can use the `\G` assertion and use this Java code snippet:

```
input = input.replaceAll("\\G,", "-");
```

Since `\G` matches the start of the line the first time, it will assert the position just before the first comma. Subsequently, it matches the positions after each comma, since `\G` matches the positions at the end of the previous match. It will stop matching when the control reaches the digit 1. Each of these matches is replaced by a single hyphen, thus giving us the same number of hyphens in the replaced string as the number of leading commas in the original input.

Let's look at another full example to understand the use of `\G` better.

Here is a sample input:

```
{%var1%, %var2%, %var3%} {%var4%, %var5%, %var6%}
```

Our task is to replace the `%` characters with the `#` (hash) characters in the first `{ ... }` section only. We can assume that `{` and `}` are perfectly balanced. The expected output is as follows:

```
{#var1#, #var2#, #var3#} {%var4%, %var5%, %var6%}
```

Note how the output has `%` replaced with `#` in only the first pair of `{ ... }`.

Here is a code listing to solve this problem:

```java
package example.regex;
class GBoundaryMatcher
{
  public static void main (String[] args)
  {
    String input = "{%var1%, %var2%, %var3%} " +
    "{%var4%, %var5%, %var6%}";
```

```
        final String re = "(^[^{]*\\{|\\G(?!^),\\h*)%([^%]+)%";
        // now use above regex in replaceAll method
        String repl = input.replaceAll(re, "$1#$2#");
        System.out.println(repl);
    }
}
```

Here is how this regex is doing the job in this code.

We use this regex to match our pattern:

```
"(^[^{]*\\{|\\G(?!^),\\h*)%([^%]+)%"
```

The preceding regex has two groups, as follows:

```
(^[^{]*\\{|\\G(?!^),\\h*)
```

This is the captured group number one. We are using alternation to select two possible patterns here:

- `^[^{]*\\{`: This matches all text up to the first { from the start.
- `\\G(?!^),\\h*`: This matches text from the end of the previous match followed by a comma and zero or more horizontal whitespaces. `(?!^)` is a negative lookahead to avoid matching `\G` at the start position. This is needed because `\G` also successfully asserts the start of the input string in the first use.

The `%([^%]+)%` pattern is our captured group number two. It is the substring surrounded by the `%` characters.

In the replacement, we use the following:

```
$1#$2#
```

This basically puts back the first group's captured text and wraps the second captured group in # instead of % to get the required output.

Once we compile and run the preceding code, it shows the following output:

```
{#var1#, #var2#, #var3#} {%var4%, %var5%, %var6%}
```

Atomic groups

An atomic group is a non-capturing group that throws away all the alternative positions remembered by any token inside the group when the matching process exits the group after the first match of the pattern inside the group. Thus, it avoids backtracking to attempt all the alternatives present in the group.

Here is the syntax:

```
(?>regex)
```

Here, the regex may contain alternative patterns. On the other hand, a non-atomic group will allow backtracking; it will try to find the first match and then if the matching ahead fails, it will backtrack and try to find the next match in alternation, until a match for the entire expression is found or all the possibilities are exhausted.

To understand it better, let's take an example of a regular expression using a non-atomic group:

```
^foo(d|die|lish)$
```

The input string here is `foodie`.

It will match the starting pattern `foo` and then the first alternative `d`. It fails at this time because the end anchor, `$`, requires that we must be at the end of the input string, but we still have two characters, `i` and `e`, to be matched. Then, the engine attempts to match the second alternative `die`. This match operation succeeds, as the `$` anchor asserts true since the input ends there and stops matching further with a successful match returned.

 Even if we use a non-capturing group instead of a capturing group here to make it `^foo(?:d|die|lish)$`, it will have the same effect while matching.

Now, take an example of the same regular expression using an **atomic group**:

```
^foo(?>d|die|lish)$
```

Note the use of `?>` after `(` to make it an atomic non-capturing group.

Let's see what happens when we apply the preceding regex against the same input string, that is, `foodie`.

It will match the starting pattern, foo, and then its first alternative, d. It fails because the $ anchor asserts false since the input does not end at food. However, because of the use of the atomic group, the regex engine gives up immediately and doesn't backtrack. Since the regex engine throws away all the alternative positions remembered inside the atomic group, it does not attempt to match the second alternative die, which would have been a successful match for a non-atomic group. Finally, this match operation fails with no match.

You need to remember a simple but important fact that the alternation tries its alternatives from left to right and always attempts to complete the match using the leftmost alternative. Therefore, whenever listing all the options in an alternation, it is good practice to place the longest matches first and then use the other alternatives to place shorter matches.

Using this principle, we can make some small changes to our atomic group to make it work.

Here is the working regex:

```
^foo(?>lish|die|d)$
```

We have the same input string, foodie.

Note that we have the same alternatives in this atomic group but with a different order. Since d is a prefix of die, we are placing the die alternative on the left-hand side of d so that the regex engine can first attempt to match foodie before attempting food.

Here is the full code listing running these examples:

```
package example.regex;
class AtomicGroupExample
{
  public static void main (String[] args)
  {
    final String input = "foodie";
    // regex with non-atomic group
    final String nonAtomicRegex = "foo(d|die|lish)";
    // regex with an atomic group
    final String atomicRegex = "foo(?>d|die|lish)";
    // regex with an alternate atomic group with correct order
    final String atomicRegexImproved = "foo(?>lish|die|d)";
    // now execute all 3 regex against same input
    System.out.printf("%s: %s%n",
    nonAtomicRegex, input.matches(nonAtomicRegex));

    System.out.printf("%s: %s%n",
    atomicRegex, input.matches(atomicRegex));
```

```
        System.out.printf("%s: %s%n",
        atomicRegexImproved , input.matches(atomicRegexImproved));
    }
}
```

After compiling and running the code, it will generate the following output:

```
foo(?:d|die|lish): true
foo(?>d|die|lish): false
foo(?>lish|die|d): true
```

 Since the atomic group prevents the regex engine from backtracking by exiting from the evaluation of all the alternatives inside the group, the atomic group usually provides a significant gain in performance while evaluating a largely sized text with multiple options in alternation.

Lookahead assertions

Positive and negative lookahead assertions are zero-width assertions that allow for certain regular expression-based checks to be performed on the text that is ahead (or on the right-hand side) of the current position. The regex engine holds on to the current position after evaluating the lookahead pattern. We can chain multiple lookahead expressions one after another, but the regex engine does not move the control after checking all the lookaheads. Lookahead assertions can help solve some complex regex problems, which are not possible or are very difficult to solve without lookahead support. The Java regular expression engine, like many other regular expression flavors, allows the use of variable-length quantifiers such as * and + in lookahead patterns.

There are two types of lookahead assertions: positive lookahead and negative lookahead.

Positive lookahead

A positive lookahead assertion asserts true if the pattern inside the lookahead is matched.

The following is its syntax:

```
(?=...)
```

For example, \d+(?=##) asserts that there must be a string, ##, immediately after matching one or more digits.

Negative lookahead

A negative lookahead assertion asserts true if the pattern inside the lookahead is not matched.

The following is its syntax:

```
(?!...)
```

For example, abc(?!xyz) asserts that there cannot be a string, xyz, immediately after matching the string abc.

Lookbehind assertions

Positive and negative lookbehind assertions are zero-width assertions that allow for certain regex-based checks to be performed on the text that precedes (or is on the left-hand side) of the current position. The regex engine holds on to the current position after evaluating the lookbehind pattern. We can chain multiple lookbehind expressions one after another, but the regex engine does not move the control after checking all the lookbehind assertions. Lookbehind assertions can also help solve some complex problems that are not possible or are very difficult to solve without lookbehind support. Up to Java version 8, the Java regular expression engine didn't allow the use of variable-length quantifiers such as * and + in lookbehind patterns. With Java 9, the Java regex engine now allows the use of these quantifiers in lookbehind assertions.

There are two types of lookbehind assertions: positive lookbehind and negative lookbehind.

Positive lookbehind

A positive lookbehind assertion asserts true if the pattern inside the lookbehind is matched.

Here is its syntax:

```
(?<=...)
```

For example, (?<=##)\d+ asserts that there must be a ## string just before matching one or more digits.

Negative lookbehind

A negative lookbehind assertion asserts true if the pattern inside the lookbehind is not matched.

Here is its syntax:

```
(?<!...)
```

For example, `(?<!xyz)abc` asserts that there cannot be the string, `xyz`, just before matching the string, `abc`.

Here are a few important points about lookaround regex patterns:

- Lookaround patterns are atomic. Like atomic groups, once a lookaround pattern is matched, the regex engine exits immediately from that lookaround, returning just a true or false assertion.
- Lookaround patterns don't move from the current position. All patterns are evaluated from the current position. The position remains the same after the lookaround assertions are completed.
- If a regular expression uses multiple lookaround assertions next to each other, then the order of those expressions is not important.
- Lookaround patterns are usually used in complex input validations, for splitting the input before or after the specified patterns, and for finding overlapping matches.

Let's look at some examples to understand the use of lookahead and lookbehind expressions.

To match an integer number with one or more digits that doesn't allow all zeroes, we can use the following:

```
^(?!0+$)\d+$
```

`(?!0+$)` is a negative lookahead expression that will assert failure if we have one or more zeroes till the end, ahead of the current position, which is the start of the input string in our example.

Given an input text with @ characters, we need to match @ only if there is a word character at the next position. We can use a positive lookahead regex here, as follows:

```
@(?=\w)
```

Here, `(?=\w)` means a positive lookahead that asserts true when there is a word character next to @.

To match an input string that doesn't allow the string zzz anywhere, we can use a negative lookahead such as this:

```
^(?!.*zzz)
```

To match a dot that is not followed or preceded by a digit, we can use negative lookahead and negative lookbehind conditions, as follows:

```
(?<!\d)\.(?!\d)
```

Here, we are using two assertions:

- `(?<!\d)` is a negative lookbehind condition that asserts that there is no digit preceding a dot
- `(?!\d)` is a negative lookahead condition that asserts that there is no digit following a dot

This will match the dot in `ip.address`, `.net`, and `abc.` but won't match the dot in `25.78`, `12.`, and `.987`.

Next, we need to match an input that must not contain the repetition of the @, #, or % characters.

We will need to use a negative lookahead pattern that contains a capturing group and a back-reference to check repetition:

```
^(?!.*([@#%])\1)
```

`(?!.*([@#%])\1)` is a negative lookahead assertion that matches and captures the given special characters in the first capturing group. Using back-reference `\1`, we check duplication of the captured character. The pattern inside the negative lookahead `.*([@#%])\1` makes sure that we don't have a duplicated @, #, or % character at any position ahead of the current position.

Now, suppose that we need to find a search term in a long text with the following conditions:

1. The search term is at the start or preceded by a whitespace.
2. The search term is at the end or followed by a whitespace.
3. The search term may contain non-word characters as well.

To solve this, we can use a regular expression with a positive lookahead and a positive lookbehind like this:

```
(?<=^|\h)searchTerm(?=\h|$)
```

Here, `(?<=^|\h)` is a positive lookbehind that asserts that the search term is at the start position or is preceded by a horizontal whitespace.

`(?=\h|$)` is a positive lookahead that asserts that the search term is at the end position or is followed by a horizontal whitespace.

Match a string containing one or more word characters but doesn't allow any of the characters to repeat.

To solve this problem, we need to use a capturing group, back-reference, and a negative lookahead like this:

```
^(?:(\w)(?!.*\1))+$
```

Here, we are matching and capturing each character in the first captured group. Each word character is asserted by a negative lookahead `(?!.*\1)`, where `\1` is the back-reference of the first captured group. The negative lookahead `(?!.*\1)` asserts that we don't have another occurrence of the captured character in the string ahead. Finally, we wrap the whole expression in a non-capturing group to be able to use the quantifier `+` to match one or more word non-repeating characters.

Suppose we need to scan a line of text and place a colon in every third position from right to left. However, we should not place a colon at the start position.

This should convert `abcd` into `a:bcd` and `123456` will be converted to `123:456`, but `abc` must not become `:abc`.

To solve this, we can use a lookahead regex, as in this code listing:

```
package example.regex;

import java.util.regex.*;
class LookAroundExample1
```

```
{
  public static void main (String[] args)
  {
    final String[] inputs =
    {"abcd98732", "pqrn", "qwerty12345678xyz", "123"};
    final Pattern p = Pattern.compile("(?!^)(?=(.{3})+$)");
    for (String s: inputs)
    {
      Matcher m = p.matcher(s);
      System.out.printf("%s => %s%n", s, m.replaceAll(":"));
    }
  }
}
```

After running this code, we'll get the following output:

```
abcd98732 => abc:d98:732
pqrn => p:qrn
qwerty12345678xyz => qw:ert:y12:345:678:xyz
123 => 123
```

As you can see, this code places a colon in every third position, going from right to left. Let's see what happens during the matching of the regular expression:

- `(?!^)` is a negative lookahead to avoid matching at the position.
- `(?=(.{3})+$)` is a positive lookahead that finds all the positions that have one or more three-character sets, ahead of the current position. This will first match the position where the first : has to be inserted, then the second, and so on. This may at first seem like something contradicting with atomic groups and the non-backtracking behaviour of a lookahead group. But it essentially is not. It is not contradicting because the lookahead itself is not backtracking. The regular expression matching is backtracking and evaluates the lookahead assertion again and again for each and every character position.

Now, suppose that we have to replace all the commas that are outside the innermost parentheses with a semi-colon, assuming all the parentheses are balanced, not nested, and unescaped in the input text.

To solve this problem, we can use a negative lookahead expression, such as this one:

```
,(?![^()]*\))
```

This one matches a comma followed by a negative lookahead assertion that asserts false when we have a right) following zero or more characters and not containing (and). Since we know that (and) are balanced, this check ensures that we match a comma that is outside (and).

Here is the full code listing to see this regex in action:

```
package example.regex;

import java.util.regex.*;

class LookAroundExample2
{
  public static void main (String[] args)
  {
    String input = "var1,var2,var3 (var1,var2,var3) var4,var5,var6
(var4,var5,var6)";
    final Pattern p = Pattern.compile(",(?![^()]*\\))");
    Matcher m = p.matcher(input);
    System.out.printf("%s%n", m.replaceAll(";"));
  }
}
```

When we run the preceding code, it gives the following output, replacing all the commas outside the parentheses:

```
var1;var2;var3 (var1,var2,var3) var4;var5;var6 (var4,var5,var6)
```

Next, suppose that we need to validate a password string with the following constraints:

- At least one uppercase English letter
- At least one lowercase English letter
- At least one digit
- At least one special character (non-word character)
- Minimum six and maximum twelve in length
- No whitespace allowed anywhere

Here is the solution:

To check for six to twelve non-whitespace characters, we can use the following:

```
^\S{6,12}$
```

For the remaining conditions, we need to use multiple lookahead expressions, one for each condition. Let's build the lookahead patterns one by one.

To ensure that there is at least one uppercase letter in the input, we can use this lookahead assertion:

```
(?=.*[A-Z])
```

This means that we have to check for the presence of an uppercase letter after zero or more characters.

Similarly, to ensure that there is at least one lowercase letter in the input, we can use this lookahead assertion:

```
(?=.*[a-z])
```

Similarly, to ensure there is at least one digit in the input, we can use the following:

```
(?=.*\d)
```

Similarly, to ensure there is at least one non-word character in the input, we can use the following:

```
(?=.*\W)
```

As mentioned earlier, the order of these lookahead patterns does not matter, so we keep them in any order in our regular expression. Putting it all together, our final regular expression will be as follows:

```
^(?=.*[A-Z])(?=.*[a-z])(?=.*\d)(?=.*\W)\S{6,12}$
```

Here is the full Java code to make this regex work:

```java
package example.regex;

import java.util.regex.*;

class LookAroundPasswordValidation
{
  public static void main (String[] args)
  {
    // build a Pattern using our regex
    final Pattern p = Pattern.compile(
    "^(?=.*[A-Z])(?=.*[a-z])(?=.*\\d)(?=.*\\W)\\S{6,12}$" );
    // input strings to be tested against our regex
    String[] inputs = { "abZ#45", "$$$f5P###", "abc123", "xyz-7612",
    "AbC@#$qwer", "xYz@#$ 1278" };
    for (String s: inputs)
    {
      Matcher m = p.matcher( s );
      System.out.printf( "%s => %s%n", s, m.matches() );
```

```
        }
    }
}
```

After compiling and running this code, we will get the following output:

```
abZ#45 => true
$$$f5P### => true
abc123 => false
xyz-7612 => false
AbC@#$qwer => false
xYz@#$1278 => false
```

This output basically shows a `true` value for all the strings that pass all our password rules and `false`, otherwise.

Capturing text from overlapping matches

Lookahead patterns are also very useful for situations where we want to match and capture text from overlapping matches.

Let's consider the following input string as an example:

```
thathathisthathathatis
```

Suppose that we need to count the occurrence of the string, `that`, in this input, including all overlapping occurrences.

Note that there are three independent `that` substrings in the input string, but there are two additional overlapping matches that we need to match and count. Here are the start-end positions of overlapping the substring `that`:

```
Positions 0-3 3-6 10-13 13-16 16-19
```

A simple search using the regex `that` will give us a match count of three because we miss out all the overlapping matches. To be able to match the overlapping matches, we need to use the lookahead pattern because lookahead patterns are zero-length. These patterns don't consume any characters; they just assert the presence of the required text ahead, based on the patterns used inside the lookahead, and the current position doesn't change. So, the solution is to use a lookahead regex as follows:

```
(?=that)
```

Here is the full code to see this regex working in action:

```
package example.regex;
import java.util.regex.Matcher;
import java.util.regex.Pattern;
class LookaheadOverlapping
{
  public static void main (String[] args)
  {
    final String kw = "that";
    final String regex = "(?=" + kw+ ")";
    final String string = "thathathisthathathatis";
    final Pattern pattern = Pattern.compile(regex);
    final Matcher matcher = pattern.matcher(string);
    int count = 0; while (matcher.find())
    {
      System.out.printf("Start: %d\tEnd:%d%n",
      matcher.start(), matcher.start() + kw.length() -1);
      count++;
    }
    System.out.printf("Match count: %d%n", count);
  }
}
```

Once we run and compile the preceding class, we will get the following output:

```
Start: 0 End:3
Start: 3 End:6
Start: 10 End:13
Start: 13 End:16
Start: 16 End:19
Match count: 5
```

You can see from this output that all the Start, End positions of the overlapping matches and, more importantly, the count of the overlapping matches, which is 5.

Here is another code listing that finds all the three character strings that have 'a' as the middle letter and the same word character before and after the letter 'a'. For example, bab, zaz, kak, dad, 5a5, and _a_ should be matched:

```
package example.regex;
import java.util.regex.Matcher;
import java.util.regex.Pattern;
class LookaheadOverlappingMatches
{
  public static void main(String[] args)
  {
    final String regex = "(?=(\\w)a\\1)";
```

```
final String string = "5a5akaktjzazbebbobababababsab";
final Matcher matcher = Pattern.compile(regex)
.matcher(string);
int count = 0; while (matcher.find())
{
    final int start = matcher.start();
    final int end = start + 2;
    System.out.printf("Start: %2d\tEnd:%2d %s%n",
    start, end, string.substring(start,end+1));
    count++;
}
    System.out.printf("Match count: %d%n", count);
}
}
```

This code generates the following output:

```
Start:  0 End: 2 5a5
Start:  4 End: 6 kak
Start:  9 End:11 zaz
Start: 17 End:19 bab
Start: 19 End:21 bab
Start: 21 End:23 bab
Match count: 6
```

Be careful with capturing groups inside a lookahead or lookbehind atomic group

You learned to use capturing groups inside lookahead or lookbehind patterns in the preceding examples. However, you must remember that lookaround expressions are zero-width atomic groups. The regex engine exits from these groups as soon as an assertion is evaluated to true or false. Due to this fact, there is no backtracking inside these groups.

Consider the following three regular expressions. The first one is without any lookahead or atomic group, the second regex uses a lookahead expression, and the third regex uses an atomic group. Note that in each of the regex patterns, we use a capturing group to match and capture zero or more word characters inside the outer group:

```
# (?:(\w*))\w*_\1
# (?=(\w*))\w*_\1
# (?>(\w*))\w*_\1
```

Suppose that we apply the preceding three regex patterns against the following input:

```
#abc_abc
```

The first regex, `#(?:(\w+)).*_\1`, will find a successful match with `group 1` as `"abc"`. Next, it matches _ and back-references `\1` to complete the match. Since the capturing group `(\w*)` initially matches the complete input, `"abc_abc"`, the regex engine backtracks multiple times to make this a successful match.

The second regex will fail to match because `(\w+)` inside the lookahead will match and capture `"abc_abc"`, and when the regex engine exits the lookahead group, it is not able to find a match with `.*_\1`, as there is no further input and the engine won't backtrack to complete the match like it does in the first regex.

The third regex with an atomic group will also fail to match due to the same reason; the regex engine won't backtrack after matching the string inside an atomic group.

Lookbehind limitations in Java regular expressions

Like many other regular expression engines, the Java regex engine does not allow a variable-length text without an obvious maximum length match in the lookbehind regex pattern. This means that we cannot use the * or + quantifiers in a lookbehind pattern. However, the Java regex engine allows for limited or finite repetition in a lookbehind regex. This gives us a workaround for doing so in Java regular expressions by using limiting quantifiers in lookbehind expressions.

This means that we cannot use the following lookbehind regex to check filenames ending with extensions:

```
(?<=\w\.\w+)$
```

However, we could change the preceding pattern to the following with a finite repetition, and now this pattern will be allowed by the Java regex engine:

```
(?<=\w\.\w{1,99})$
```

However, it limits the number of word characters in the lookbehind after the dot to be from 1 to 99 instead of open-ended one or more word characters, as is the case with the + quantifier. However, you should use such a feature with caution and check the performance of the resulting regular expression. The Java lookbehind implementation also had quite a few bugs in the earlier versions. Some of these bugs have been resolved but one can still get unexpected results while using complex lookbehind regular expressions in Java.

Java 9, however, allows regex patterns without an obvious maximum-length restriction in lookbehind assertions. This will allow programmers to use the lookbehind regex patterns without any maximum length match, such as the following regex in the previous example:

```
(?<=\w\.\w+)$
```

Summary

In this chapter, we learned zero-width assertions and how they are crucial for solving some important matching problems. We discussed the boundary matcher, \G, and its usefulness in solving some problems. We discovered the idea behind atomic groups and understood how they can improve the overall regex performance. Then, we covered all the important lookahead and lookbehind patterns. We covered some interesting matching, validation, and splitting problems that are solved using lookarounds.

In the next chapter, we will continue to learn advanced concepts of Java regular expressions, such as union and intersection within character classes, and negated character classes.

7
Understanding the Union, Intersection, and Subtraction of Character Classes

Some regular expression engines allow composite character classes, or character classes inside other character classes. The Java regular expression engine also supports many of these features, and we will discuss these features in this chapter.

We will cover the following topics in this chapter:

- The union of character classes
- The intersection of character classes
- The subtraction of character classes
- The advantages of using composite character classes

The union of character classes

The union of character classes will match a character that would be matched by any of the composing character classes. Essentially, this is the definition of the union operation in general. In regular expressions, it is possible to create unions of character classes by simply writing a character class inside another.

You may remember that character classes open with the [character and close with the] character, and we can list characters and character ranges between the opening and closing brackets.

In addition to those, we can use other character sets inside the brackets, and the resulting set will be the union of all these character classes. This way, there is no union operator to create the composition of these character classes; we just simply write them inside each other.

For example, consider the following composite character class:

```
[A-D[PQR]]
```

This matches any character in the range of A to D or any single character P, Q, or R. This regular expression can also be written as follows:

```
[A-DPQR]
```

We can also create a union of more than two character classes, such as as in the following regular expression:

```
[A-D[P-S][X-Z]]
```

This matches any character in the range of A to D, any character in the range of P to S, or any character in the range from X to Z. This regular expression can also be written as follows:

```
[A-DP-SX-Z]
```

The union of character classes can also be used with a negated inner character class, and this is where character class unions really start to shine and give us extra value. We get to see a good use of the union operation only when we use the union of various character classes with a negated character class.

Let's consider, for example, the following code listing on the union with a negated character class:

```
package example.regex;

import java.util.regex.*;
public class UnionExample
{
  public static void main(String[] args)
  {
    final String re = "[#@.[^\\p{Punct}\\s]]";
    final String[] arr = new String[] {
      "A", "#", "@", "1", "5", " ", "\n", ":", ".", "a", "%", "-", "3"
    };
    for (String s: arr)
    {
    System.out.printf("[%s] %s%n", s,
    (s.matches(re) ? "matches" : "does not match"));
```

```
      }
    }
  }
```

This regex has the following negated character class:

```
[^\\p{Punct}\\s]
```

The preceding negated character class allows any character that is not a punctuation and not a space character. Now, suppose that we want to allow a few selected punctuation characters, @, #, and ., or in other words, the [@#.] character class. In this scenario, the union comes handy. We make a composite character class that uses a union of both these cases, as follows:

```
[#@.[^\\p{Punct}\\s]]
```

Now, this composite character class will allow the [@#.] characters, or any character that is not a punctuation and not a space character.

Once we compile and run the preceding code, we'll get the following output:

```
[A] matches
[#] matches
[@] matches
[1] matches
[5] matches
[ ] does not match
[
] does not match
[:] does not match
[.] matches
[a] matches
[%] does not match
[-] does not match
[3] matches
```

You can see the output of "matches" for all the character sets that are not included inside our negated character class or allowed by the [#@.] character class. It returns "does not match" for all other cases.

The intersection of character classes

The intersection operation on character classes results in a composite class that contains every character allowed by **all** of its operand (inner) classes or, in other words, matches characters that belong to all the character classes in the composite character class pattern. The intersection operator is as follows:

```
&&
```

For example, consider the following composite character class using the `&&` operator:

```
[A-Z&&[PQR]]
```

This matches any character that is in the range of A to Z and is one of the single P, Q, or R characters. However, the preceding regular expression can also be simply written as follows:

```
[PQR]
```

The following composite character class using intersection matches the digits, 5 and 6, since only these two digits belong to all the three character classes:

```
[1-7&&[3-6]&&[5-8]]
```

To see this regex in action, let's use this complete code:

```java
package example.regex;

import java.util.regex.*;
public class IntersectionExample
{
  public static void main(String[] args)
  {
    final Pattern p = Pattern.compile("[1-7&&[3-6]&&[5-8]]");
    for (int i=0; i<10; i++)
    {
      String s = String.valueOf(i);
      Matcher m = p.matcher(s);
       System.out.printf("[%s] %s%n", s,
          (m.matches() ? "matches" : "does not match"));
    }
  }
}
```

When we compile and run the preceding code, we will see the following output:

```
[0] does not match
[1] does not match
[2] does not match
[3] does not match
[4] does not match
[5] matches
[6] matches
[7] does not match
[8] does not match
[9] does not match
```

As you can see, it shows "matches" only for the digits, 5 and 6.

Let's take another example, which involves matching a non-whitespace character that is not a Unicode letter. We know we can use the following regex using a positive lookahead:

```
(?=\S)\P{L}
```

We can also use an intersection operation to write this example, as follows:

```
[\\S&&[\\P{L}]]
```

Due to the use of the && operator here, it matches a character that satisfies both the properties, \S (non-whitespace) and \P{L} (non-letters).

Note that the inner square brackets are optional when not using a negated character class in an intersection operation. Hence, the preceding regex can also be written as follows:

```
[\\S&&\\P{L}]
```

Similarly, to match an uppercase Greek letter, we can use the intersection of the following two classes:

- \p{InGreek}: This matches a character in the Greek block
- \p{Lu}: This matches an uppercase Unicode letter

By combining these two character classes with intersection, we can make a single composite character class, as follows:

```
[\p{InGreek}&&[\p{Lu}]]
```

To test the preceding regex, let's pick some Greek letters and write a simple Java code, such as the following, to test our regex against the selected Greek letters:

```
package example.regex;

import java.util.regex.*;
public class UppercaseGreekIntersectionExample
{
  public static void main(String[] args)
  {
    final Pattern p = Pattern.compile("[\\p{InGreek}&&[\\p{Lu}]]");
    final String[] arr = new String[] {
      "Γ", "Δ", "Θ", "Ξ", "Π", "Σ", "Φ", "α", "β", "γ", "δ", "ε", "A", "P",
"e", "r"
    };

    for (String s: arr)
    {
      Matcher m = p.matcher(s);
      System.out.printf("[%s] %s%n", s,
          (m.matches() ? "matches" : "does not match"));
    }
  }
}
```

When we run the preceding class, it prints the following output:

```
[Γ] matches
[Δ] matches
[Θ] matches
[Ξ] matches
[Π] matches
[Σ] matches
[Φ] matches
[α] does not match
[β] does not match
[γ] does not match
[δ] does not match
[ε] does not match
[A] does not match
[P] does not match
[e] does not match
[r] does not match
```

As you can see, "matches" is only printed for the uppercase Greek letters. For all the other letters, it prints "does not match".

The subtraction of character classes

Suppose we have to match characters that belong to one class but not to another in a composite character class pattern. There is no separate operator for the subtraction operation. Subtraction is performed by using the intersection operator, &&, and a negated inner character class.

> A regular expression is usually more readable if we write the larger set in front and the one we want to subtract from it after the && operator.

For example, consider the following composite character class:

    [0-9&&[^3-6]]

It will match the digits, 0 to 9, except the digits, 3 to 6. This character class can also be written as a union of two character classes:

    [[0-2][7-9]]

We can also just use a simple character class, as follows:

    [0-27-9]

In order to match all the English consonant uppercase letters, we can subtract five vowels from uppercase letters, such as in the following regex:

    [A-Z&&[^AEIOU]]

We can also reverse the order of the two sets used in the preceding regex and use the following regex:

    [[^AEIOU]&&A-Z]

Suppose we want to match all punctuation characters except four basic math operators: +, -, *, and /. We can use the following composite character class using the subtraction operation:

    [\p{Punct}&&[^+*/-]]

Here is a test class that tests the preceding subtraction character class:

```
package example.regex;

import java.util.regex.*;
public class SubtractionExample
{
  public static void main(String[] args)
  {
    final Pattern p = Pattern.compile("[\\p{Punct}&&[^+*/-]]");
    final String[] arr = new String[] {
      "!", "@", "#", "$", "%", "+", "-", "*", "/", "1", "M", "d"
    };

    for (String s: arr)
    {
      Matcher m = p.matcher(s);
      System.out.printf("[%s] %s%n", s,
          (m.matches() ? "matches" : "does not match"));
    }
  }
}
```

This program produces the following output when we run it after compilation:

```
[!] matches
[@] matches
[#] matches
[$] matches
[%] matches
[+] does not match
[-] does not match
[*] does not match
[/] does not match
[1] does not match
[M] does not match
[d] does not match
```

As is evident from this output, it allows all the punctuation characters except the four listed math operators.

Why should you use composite character classes?

We should use composite character classes for the following reasons:

- To create new custom character classes from predefined Unicode blocks. For example, to match all the letters in an Arabic Unicode block, we can use the following:

```
[\p{InArabic}&&\p{L}]
```

- To avoid potentially slower lookahead or lookbehind patterns by using the intersection or subtraction operation on multiple character classes.
- To enhance the readability of the regular expression.

Summary

In this chapter, we discussed composite and inner character classes. We found out how we can use the union, intersection, and subtraction operations to combine simple character classes and make a completely different character class to suit our requirements. You learned some good usage patterns of composite character classes for solving tricky problems. Note how we could avoid more complex lookahead and lookbehind assertions by using the union and intersection of character classes.

In the next chapter, we will discuss the pitfalls of some poorly written regular expressions, and you will learn ways to avoid them. You will also learn some important optimizing tips and performance improvement methods for writing complex regular expressions.

8

Regular Expression Pitfalls, Optimization, and Performance Improvements

Regular expressions, if not written well may perform poorly. They may run slowly, and when they are executed frequently in some code, they may be the source of high CPU utilization. To avoid these problems, regular expressions have to be crafted carefully, understanding the possible pitfalls, and they also have to be tested thoroughly. We will be covering the following topics in this chapter:

- Common pitfalls and ways to avoid them while writing regular expressions
- How to test your regex functionality and performance
- Optimization and performance enhancing tips
- Catastrophic backtracking and how to avoid it

Common pitfalls and ways to avoid them while writing regular expressions

Let's discuss some common mistakes people make while building regular expressions to solve various problems.

Do not forget to escape regex metacharacters outside a character class

You learned that all the special metacharacters, such as *, +, ?, ., |, (,), [, {, ^, $, and so on, need to be escaped if the intent is to match them literally. I often see cases where programmers leave them unescaped, thus giving a totally different meaning to the regular expression. The Java regex API that we discussed in Chapter 5, *Introduction to Java Regular Expressions APIs - Pattern and Matcher Classes*, throws a non-checked exception if a regex pattern is wrongly formatted and cannot be compiled.

Avoid escaping every non-word character

Some programmers overdo escaping, thinking that they need to escape every non-word character such as colon, hyphen, semicolon, forward slash, and whitespace, which is not correct. They end up writing a regular expression as follows:

```
^https?\:\/\/(www\.)?example\.com$
```

The preceding regex pattern uses excessive escaping. This pattern still works, but it is not very readable. The colon and forward slash have no special meaning in regex; hence, it is better to write this regex in the following way:

```
^https?://(www\.)?example\.com$
```

Avoid unnecessary capturing groups to reduce memory consumption

We come across so many examples of regular expressions on the internet that promote unnecessary capturing groups. If we are not extracting any substring or not using a group in backreferences, then it is better to avoid capturing groups by using one or more of the following ways:

1. We can use character classes in certain cases. Consider the following capturing group:

   ```
   (a|e|i|o|u)
   ```

   So, instead of using the preceding regex, we can use the following:

   ```
   [aeiou]
   ```

2. We can use a non-capturing group by placing a `?:` at the start of the group. Consider the following regex:

```
(red|blue|white)
```

Instead of the previous regex, we can use the following:

```
(?:red|blue|white)
```

3. To write a regex to match an integer or decimal number there is no need to use the following regex:

```
^(\d*)(\.?)(\d+)$
```

We can just rewrite it by removing unnecessary groups, as follows:

```
^\d*\.?d+$
```

4. Sometimes, a regex may contain multiple problems, such as the ones we discussed in the previous subsection:

```
^https?\:\/\/(www\.)?example\.com$
```

Not only does this regex use excessive escaping but there is also an unnecessary capturing group in this regex. Hence, by applying these fixes, the preceding regex can be better written as follows:

```
^https?://(?:www\.)?example\.com$
```

However, don't forget to use the required group around alternation

Often, we see regex patterns that use alternation, and around the alternation, we use anchors or boundary matchers without safeguarding the alternation expression in a group. Note that the `^`, `$`, `\A`, `\Z`, `\z` anchors and the `\b` boundary matcher have a higher precedence than the alternation character, `|` (pipe)

So, consider a regular expression written as follows:

```
^com|org|net$
```

It will also match `computer`, `organization`, and `internet`, though the intent probably was to match only `com`, `net`, and `org`. This is because the start anchor, `^`, is being applied to `com` only and the end anchor, `$`, is being applied to `net`, whereas `org` is not anchored at all.

This regular expression should be written as follows to match only `com`, `org`, and `net` correctly:

```
^(?:com|org|net)$
```

Use predefined character classes instead of longer versions

We discussed predefined character classes and Unicode character classes in `Chapter 2`, *Understanding the Core Concepts of Java Regular Expressions*. We need to make good use of it. So use `\d` instead of `[0-9]` or `\D` instead of `[^0-9]`, and use `\w` instead of `[a-zA-Z_0-9]` or `\W` instead of `[^a-zA-Z_0-9]`.

Use the limiting quantifier instead of repeating a character or pattern multiple times

The MAC address of a computer is a unique identifier assigned to network interfaces at the time of manufacturing. MAC addresses are 6 bytes or 48 bits in length and are written in the `nn:nn:nn:nn:nn:nn` format, where each n represents a hexadecimal digit. To match a MAC address, one can write the following regex:

```
^[A-F0-9]{2}:[A-F0-9]{2}:[A-F0-9]{2}:[A-F0-9]{2}:[A-F0-9]{2}:[A-F0-9]{2}$
```

However, it is much cleaner and more readable to write the regex as follows:

```
^(?:[A-F\d]{2}:){5}[A-F\d]{2}$
```

Note how short and readable this regex pattern has become when compared to the previous regex.

Do not use an unescaped hyphen in the middle of a character class

We know that most of the special regex metacharacters are treated literally inside the character class and we do not need to escape them inside the character class. However, if an unescaped hyphen is used between two characters, then it makes it a range between the previous and the next character of the hyphen.

As an illustrative example, let's consider this character class expression to match the four basic math operators, +,−,*,/:

```
[*+-/]
```

The way it is written, this character class has a hyphen between the + and / characters. This makes the character class match all the characters that fall between + (0x2A) and / (0x2F), as per the ASCII table. Due to this reason, the preceding pattern will also match the comma (,), that is, 0x2C, and DOT (.), that is, 0x2E, characters.

An unescaped hyphen can be safely used at the first or last positions in a character class to avoid making a range. With that in mind, we can correct this character class by using any of the following forms:

```
[-*+/]
[*+/-]
[*+\-/]
```

The mistake of calling matcher.goup() without a prior call to matcher.find(), matcher.matches(), or matcher.lookingAt()

This annoying mistake is found in many programs. As the heading says, these are cases where programmers call any of the group() methods without a prior call to the find, matches, or lookingAt methods. A matcher is created using the pattern.matcher(String) method call, but we need to invoke one of these three methods to perform a match operation.

If we call `matcher.group()` without calling one of these three methods, then the code will throw a `java.lang.IllegalStateException` exception, as the following code is doing:

```
package example.regex;
import java.util.regex.*;
public class MissingMethodCall
{
  public static void main(String[] args)
  {
    final Pattern p = Pattern.compile("(\\d*)\\.?(\\d+)");
    final String input = "123.75";
    Matcher m = p.matcher(input);
    System.out.printf("Number Value [%s], Decimal Value [%s]%n",
    m.group(1), m.group(2));
  }
}
```

Note that the code calls `m.group(1)` and `m.group(2)` right after it instantiates the matcher object from a pattern instance. Once compiled and executed, this code will throw an unwanted `java.lang.IllegalStateException` exception, indicating that the matcher instance is not in the correct state to return group information.

In order to fix this code, insert a call to any one of the three methods (`find`, `matches`, or `lookingAt`) to perform a match operation, as shown in the following code:

```
package example.regex;

import java.util.regex.*;

public class RightMethodCall
{
  public static void main(String[] args)
  {
    final Pattern p = Pattern.compile("(\\d*)\\.?(\\d+)");
    final String input = "123.75";

    Matcher m = p.matcher(input);
    if (m.find()) // or m.lookingAt() or m.matches()
    {
      System.out.printf("Integer Part [%s], Fractional Part [%s]%n",
      m.group(1), m.group(2));
    }
  }
}
```

Now, this code will produce the correct output, as follows:

```
Integer Part [123], Fractional Part [75]
```

Do not use regular expressions to parse XML / HTML data

Using regular expressions to parse XML or HTML text is probably the most frequently committed mistake. Although regular expressions are very useful, they have their limitations and these limits are usually met when trying to use them for XML or HTML parsing. HTML and XML are not regular languages by nature.

Luckily, there are other tools in Java for that purpose. The JDK contains readily available classes to parse these formats and convert them to **Document Object Model (DOM)**, or to work with them on the fly using the SAX parsing model.

Do not use regular expressions for certain tasks when there are more specific parsers for the purpose. The fact that there are other readily available tools gives you a hint that probably regular expressions, in such a case, are not the best tools. After all, that is the reason why the programmers of the XML and HTML parsers started their work.

How to test and benchmark your regular expression performance

There are several free online regular expression tools available that tell you the number of steps to match a regex pattern against a given set of inputs and also provide you valuable debug info. You should also write your unit test cases. Here is a list of some online tools that can be used:

- Use jshell available with Java 9 to quickly test your regex
- Use RegexMatchers, a utility class with static methods, to test your regex in JUnit; check http://matchers.jcabi.com/regex-matchers.html
- regex101.com
- www.regexplanet.com
- www.rexegg.com
- www.debuggex.com
- regexper.com

- regexbuddy.com (not free)
- Use the Java/JUnit regex-tester library from
  https://github.com/nickawatts/regex-tester

In addition to these tools, you can yourself write your own comprehensive unit test cases using JUnit in your favorite Java IDE and check the timings and other matching information.

Here is an example of JUnit code using the RegExMatchers library:

```
package example.regex;
import com.jcabi.matchers.RegexMatchers;
import org.hamcrest.MatcherAssert;
import org.junit.Test;

public class RegexTest
{
  @Test
  public void matchesDecimalNumberPattern()
  {
    MatcherAssert.assertThat(
      "[+-]?\\d*\\.?\\d+",
      RegexMatchers.matchesPattern("-145.78")
    );
  }
}
```

You are encouraged to use this library to build your own test cases and ensure that your regex passes all the edge cases.

Catastrophic or exponential backtracking

Regular expression engines can be broadly categorized into two types:

1. The **Non-deterministic Finite Automation (NFA)** engine
2. The **Deterministic Finite Automation (DFA)** engine

The DFA engines do not evaluate each character more than once to find a match. On the other hand, the NFA engines support backtracking, which means that each character in the input can be evaluated multiple times by the regex engine. The Java regular expression engine is an NFA engine.

Regex engines backtrack or give back one position at a time to make various attempts to match a given pattern when using the greedy quantifier or trying alternations. Similarly, when using lazy quantifiers, the regex engine moves forward one position at a time to attempt matching.

Regex engines usually take less time to find a positive match in the given input as compared to returning a failure for a non-match. The NFA regex engines need to evaluate all the possible permutations before returning a failure.

For example, in a regular expression that uses nested repetition quantifiers, the regex engine backtracks excessively while matching a long input text. A catastrophic backtracking problem usually occurs when the regex engine fails to make a negative match towards the end of the string and after attempting far too many permutations.

As an example, check the following regex with nested quantifiers:

```
^(\w+)*$
```

Suppose we test it against an input text that does not have a word character in the end, such as this input string:

```
abcdefghijklmno:
```

We know that due to the presence of a non-word character (colon) at the end of the input, the match will fail. However, due to the presence of nested compound quantifiers, `(\w+)*`, the regex engine backtracks excessively and makes a lot of attempts to match the input before giving up.

Excessive backtracking may also be caused by two or more alternatives that are mutually exclusive and can match the same string in the input. For example, having a regex pattern like this one to match the text between the `%%` tags:

```
%%(.|\s)+%%
```

This regex may also cause catastrophic backtracking for failed cases, such as the following input string with a missing closing tag:

```
%%          something     here     abcd     123
```

The problem here is that the alternations in `(.|\s)` are not mutually exclusive, as dot can also match the same whitespace that is matched by `\s`, except the newline character.

Here is a complete program listing that demonstrates a dynamically building regex getting slower with every iteration of the loop and eventually causing catastrophic backtracking:

```
package example.regex;
import java.util.regex.Matcher;
import java.util.regex.Pattern;
public class CatastropicBacktracking
{
  public static void main(String[] args)
  {
    final int MAX = 30;
    for (int i = 1; i < MAX; i++)
    {
      StringBuilder sb1 = new StringBuilder(i);
      StringBuilder sb2 = new StringBuilder(i);
      for (int j = i; j > 0; j--)
      {
        sb1.append('a');
        sb2.append("a?");
      }
      sb2.append(sb1);
      final Pattern p = Pattern.compile("^" + sb2.toString() + "$");
      Matcher m = p.matcher(sb1.toString());
      long start = System.nanoTime();
      m.matches();
      long end = System.nanoTime();
      System.out.printf("%s:: ( %sms ) :: Pattern <%s>,
      Input <%s>%n", i, (end - start)/1_000_000, sb2, sb1);
    }
  }
}
```

When you compile and run the preceding program and look at the generated output, you will note an output as follows:

```
1:: ( 0ms ) :: Pattern <a?a>, Input <a>
2:: ( 0ms ) :: Pattern <a?a?aa>, Input <aa>
3:: ( 0ms ) :: Pattern <a?a?a?aaa>, Input <aaa>
4:: ( 0ms ) :: Pattern <a?a?a?a?aaaa>, Input <aaaa>
5:: ( 0ms ) :: Pattern <a?a?a?a?a?aaaaa>, Input <aaaaa>
6:: ( 0ms ) :: Pattern <a?a?a?a?a?a?aaaaaa>, Input <aaaaaa>
7:: ( 0ms ) :: Pattern <a?a?a?a?a?a?a?aaaaaaa>, Input <aaaaaaa>
8:: ( 0ms ) :: Pattern <a?a?a?a?a?a?a?a?aaaaaaaa>, Input <aaaaaaaa>
9:: ( 0ms ) :: Pattern <a?a?a?a?a?a?a?a?a?aaaaaaaaa>, Input <aaaaaaaaa>
10:: ( 0ms ) :: Pattern <a?a?a?a?a?a?a?a?a?a?aaaaaaaaaa>, Input
<aaaaaaaaaa>
11:: ( 0ms ) :: Pattern <a?a?a?a?a?a?a?a?a?a?a?aaaaaaaaaaa>, Input
```

```
<aaaaaaaaaa>
12:: ( 0ms ) :: Pattern <a?a?a?a?a?a?a?a?a?a?a?a?aaaaaaaaaaaa>, Input
<aaaaaaaaaaaa>
13:: ( 10ms ) :: Pattern <a?a?a?a?a?a?a?a?a?a?a?a?a?a?aaaaaaaaaaaaa>, Input
<aaaaaaaaaaaaa>
14:: ( 1ms ) :: Pattern <a?a?a?a?a?a?a?a?a?a?a?a?a?a?aaaaaaaaaaaaaa>, Input
<aaaaaaaaaaaaaa>
15:: ( 15ms ) :: Pattern <a?a?a?a?a?a?a?a?a?a?a?a?a?a?a?aaaaaaaaaaaaaaa>,
Input <aaaaaaaaaaaaaaa>
16:: ( 18ms ) :: Pattern
<a?a?a?a?a?a?a?a?a?a?a?a?a?a?a?a?aaaaaaaaaaaaaaaa>, Input
<aaaaaaaaaaaaaaaa>
17:: ( 29ms ) :: Pattern
<a?a?a?a?a?a?a?a?a?a?a?a?a?a?a?a?a?aaaaaaaaaaaaaaaaa>, Input
<aaaaaaaaaaaaaaaaa>
18:: ( 22ms ) :: Pattern
<a?a?a?a?a?a?a?a?a?a?a?a?a?a?a?a?a?a?aaaaaaaaaaaaaaaaaa>, Input
<aaaaaaaaaaaaaaaaaa>
19:: ( 51ms ) :: Pattern
<a?a?a?a?a?a?a?a?a?a?a?a?a?a?a?a?a?a?a?aaaaaaaaaaaaaaaaaaa>, Input
<aaaaaaaaaaaaaaaaaaa>
20:: ( 97ms ) :: Pattern
<a?a?a?a?a?a?a?a?a?a?a?a?a?a?a?a?a?a?a?a?aaaaaaaaaaaaaaaaaaaa>, Input
<aaaaaaaaaaaaaaaaaaaa>
21:: ( 188ms ) :: Pattern
<a?a?a?a?a?a?a?a?a?a?a?a?a?a?a?a?a?a?a?a?a?aaaaaaaaaaaaaaaaaaaaa>, Input
<aaaaaaaaaaaaaaaaaaaaa>
22:: ( 441ms ) :: Pattern
<a?a?a?a?a?a?a?a?a?a?a?a?a?a?a?a?a?a?a?a?a?a?aaaaaaaaaaaaaaaaaaaaaa>, Input
<aaaaaaaaaaaaaaaaaaaaaa>
23:: ( 1003ms ) :: Pattern
<a?a?a?a?a?a?a?a?a?a?a?a?a?a?a?a?a?a?a?a?a?a?a?aaaaaaaaaaaaaaaaaaaaaaa>,
Input <aaaaaaaaaaaaaaaaaaaaaaa>
24:: ( 1549ms ) :: Pattern
<a?a?a?a?a?a?a?a?a?a?a?a?a?a?a?a?a?a?a?a?a?a?a?a?aaaaaaaaaaaaaaaaaaaaaaaa>,
Input <aaaaaaaaaaaaaaaaaaaaaaaa>
25:: ( 3010ms ) :: Pattern
<a?a?a?a?a?a?a?a?a?a?a?a?a?a?a?a?a?a?a?a?a?a?a?a?a?aaaaaaaaaaaaaaaaaaaaaaaa
a>, Input <aaaaaaaaaaaaaaaaaaaaaaaaa>
26:: ( 5884ms ) :: Pattern
<a?a?a?a?a?a?a?a?a?a?a?a?a?a?a?a?a?a?a?a?a?a?a?a?a?a?aaaaaaaaaaaaaaaaaaaaaa
aaaa>, Input <aaaaaaaaaaaaaaaaaaaaaaaaaa>
27:: ( 12588ms ) :: Pattern
<a?a?a?a?a?a?a?a?a?a?a?a?a?a?a?a?a?a?a?a?a?a?a?a?a?a?a?aaaaaaaaaaaaaaaaaaaa
aaaaaaa>, Input <aaaaaaaaaaaaaaaaaaaaaaaaaaa>
28:: ( 24765ms ) :: Pattern
<a?a?a?a?a?a?a?a?a?a?a?a?a?a?a?a?a?a?a?a?a?a?a?a?a?a?a?a?aaaaaaaaaaaaaaaaaa
aaaaaaaaaa>, Input <aaaaaaaaaaaaaaaaaaaaaaaaaaaa>
```

```
29:: ( 51679ms ) :: Pattern
<a?a?a?a?a?a?a?a?a?a?a?a?a?a?a?a?a?a?a?a?a?a?a?a?a?a?a?a?a?aaaaaaaaaaaaaaaa
aaaaaaaaaaaaa>, Input <aaaaaaaaaaaaaaaaaaaaaaaaaaaaaa>
```

Note how the execution time grows rapidly on higher values of the counter i, especially after 25.

How to avoid catastrophic backtracking

Here are some tips to keep in mind while handling situations with catastrophic or excessive backtracking in your regex:

- When you write regular expressions, make sure they fail fast without spending a lot of unnecessary steps in backtracking.
- When using nested repetition operators or quantifiers, make sure that there is only one unique way to match the a string.
- Make good judicious use of atomic groups and possessive quantifiers to avoid excessive backtracking.
- You should avoid having too many optional matches that are not mutually exclusive in an alternation pattern.
- Be very careful when using a free-flowing pattern such as .* or .+ in your regex. Wherever possible, use negated character classes for cutting down the backtracking steps and for better performance.
- Avoid matching hugely sized text using a single regex. It is better to match smaller strings using your regex and call `matcher.find()` in a loop to get multiple matches. If needed, use another inner pattern to match and examine the matches found by the main pattern.

The regex with the nested quantifier that caused catastrophic backtracking is as follows:

```
^(\w+)*$
```

We can make use of possessive quantifiers to disallow any backtracking, as follows:

```
^(\w+)*+$
```

You will note a massive jump in this improved regex in any of the benchmarks or regex testing tools, as suggested earlier.

Also, in the alternation regex example, we found that this regex causes excessive backtracking for failed cases:

```
%%(.|\s)%%
```

It can be converted to the following regex to avoid excessive backtracking:

```
%%(\S|\s)+%%
```

It is even better to avoid the group and use a character class, as follows:

```
%%[\S\s]+%%
```

Note the use of `\s` instead of dot to make alternatives mutually exclusive.

A regex that can cause excessive backtracking is as follows:

```
^(?:.*:)+#$
```

In the preceding regex example, if we use a negated character class instead of `.*`, then we can avoid catastrophic backtracking:

```
^(?:[^:]+:)+#$
```

The regex engine doesn't backtrack excessively because the negated character class, `[^:]`, matches any character except a colon instead of the dot that matches everything, including the colon.

Consider another example with this regex pattern that has the nested repetition operator, `+`:

```
%(?:[p-s]+|ye|wo)+%
```

This regex pattern attempts to match a string that starts with the following conditions:

- Must start with %
- % must be followed by one or more alternations: letters p,q,r,s or the string ye or wo
- Must end with another %

Now test this regex pattern against the input string, as follows:

```
%yeqpsrwospqr
```

Obviously, the regex pattern is not going to match because the last % is missing. However, note that the starting % and all the following letters will match the regex pattern before the last %. Due to this, the regex engine will backtrack several times while making attempts to match the complete input before finally giving up.

When testing this regex on the *regex101* website's debugger, it shows the following:

```
match 1 failed in 748 steps
```

748 may be a quite a big number for the number of steps taken to fail the match for a small-sized input. Regex patterns such as this can slow down your application considerably. Some of them can even hang your code for many hours or days due to the catastrophic backtracking behavior.

Now, to prevent this catastrophic backtracking behavior, let's consider the two options the we recommended earlier:

1. Use a possessive quantifier, as follows:

```
%(?:[p-s]+|ye|wo)++%
```

On testing the preceding pattern on the same site, we get the following in the debugger:

```
match 1 failed in 33 steps
```

2. Use an atomic group, as follows:

```
%(?>[p-s]+|ye|wo)+%
```

On testing the preceding pattern on the same site, we get the following in the debugger:

```
match 1 failed in 36 steps
```

You can notice that by using any of the aforementioned techniques, we make the regex engine fail sooner and avoid the unnecessarily high number of backtracking steps.

Optimization and performance enhancement tips

Let's discuss some optimization techniques and performance enhancement guidelines.

Use a compiled form of regular expressions

Compile your string regex pattern using the `Pattern.compile(String)` method call followed by calls to the Matcher APIs instead of calling shorthand methods in string, such as `matches()`, `replaceAll`, and `replaceFirst`, especially when these matching or replacement methods are invoked repeatedly inside a loop. Repeated calls to `String.matches()` or any other regex-based method defined in the String API will compile the String regex pattern every time; this can be very time-consuming for a complex regex pattern.

Use a negated character class instead of the greedy and slow .* or .+

Wherever possible, use negated character classes instead of the potential performance draining patterns (`.*` or `.+`), as follows:

```
param1=[^&]+&param2=[^&]+&param3=[^&]+$
```

Avoid using slow-performing quantifiers, as follows:

```
param1=.+&param2=.+param3=.+$
```

Avoid unnecessary grouping

Avoiding unnecessary captured groups in your regex. If grouping is required in your regex, then use non-capturing groups to save the overall memory footprint of the regex pattern while executing.

Use lazy quantifiers strategically instead of greedy quantifiers that cause excessive backtracking

Suppose we need to match an input that contains three complete words, *start*, *middle*, and *end*, separated by non-whitespace characters.

Consider using the following pattern with a lazy quantifier:

```
\bstart\b\S+?\bmiddle\b\S+?\bend\b
```

Instead of using the following pattern, our match will be faster if we use the preceding pattern:

```
\bstart\b\S+\bmiddle\b\S+\bend\b
```

Make use of possessive quantifiers to avoid backtracking

Recall that we discussed in an earlier chapter how a possessive quantifier is used for fail-fast paradigm. Wherever possible, make good use of possessive quantifiers to tell the regex engine to avoid backtracking.

Suppose we need to write a regex to match the text between two markers, @START@ and @END@. It is given that the semicolon is now allowed between two markers.

We can write this regex with the + or greedy quantifier, as follows:

```
@START@[^;]+@END@
```

However, it is better to use the ++ or possessive quantifier in the regex, as follows:

```
@START@[^;]++@END@
```

This regex will be faster to execute for failed matches, such as the following string:

```
@START@ abc 123 foo @XYZ@
```

Extract common repeating substrings out of alternation

Consider the following pattern:

```
(playground|player|playing)
```

Instead of using the preceding pattern, it is better to extract the common substring, play, and move it to the left of alternation, as follows:

```
play(ground|er|ing)
```

Use atomic group to avoid backtracking and fail fast

Recall from Chapter 6, *Exploring Zero-Width Assertions, Lookarounds, and Atomic Groups*, that an atomic group is a non-capturing group that exits the group and throws away all the alternative positions remembered by any token inside the group, after the first match of the pattern inside the group. Thus, it avoids backtracking to attempt all the alternatives present in the group.

Due to this very characteristic of atomic groups, the use of atomic groups in certain scenarios saves many unnecessary backtracking steps and speeds up the overall regex execution.

So, use this atomic group:

```
\btra(?>ck|ce|ining|de|in|nsit|ns|uma)\b
```

It is better to use the preceding atomic group instead of the following non-capturing group:

```
\btra(?:ck|ce|ining|de|in|nsit|ns|uma)\b
```

The difference in behavior will be evident when matching an input string, such as *tracker*, which fails to match.

Summary

In the final chapter of this book, we discussed some common mistakes people make while writing regular expressions. These mistakes often cause some exceptions to be thrown at runtime or cause the regular expressions to fail the match unexpectedly. Then, you learned the various ways to avoid such mistakes.

We discussed catastrophic backtracking in regular expressions and the tricks to avoid excessive backtracking. By minimizing the backtracking steps, regular expressions can become really efficient.

You learned the testing and benchmarking techniques for regular expressions. Finally, we covered many regex optimization and performance enhancing tips in detail. We hope these tips help you understand the building blocks of regular expressions and write better-performing regular expressions to solve complex parsing and matching problems.

Index

Made in the USA
San Bernardino, CA
03 June 2019